ARE GOVERNMENT ORGANIZATIONS
IMMORTAL?

ARE GOVERNMENT ORGANIZATIONS IMMORTAL?

Herbert Kaufman

THE BROOKINGS INSTITUTION
Washington, D.C.

Copyright © 1976 by

THE BROOKINGS INSTITUTION

1775 Massachusetts Avenue, N.W., Washington, D.C. 20036

Library of Congress Cataloging in Publication Data:

Kaufman, Herbert, 1922–
    Are government organizations immortal?

    Includes bibliographical references.
  1. United States—Executive departments.
  2. United States—Politics and government—20th century.
  I. Title.
JK21.K37   353.04   75-43466
ISBN 0-8157-4839-6

1 2 3 4 5 6 7 8 9

THE BROOKINGS INSTITUTION is an independent organization devoted to nonpartisan research, education, and publication in economics, government, foreign policy, and the social sciences generally. Its principal purposes are to aid in the development of sound public policies and to promote public understanding of issues of national importance.

The Institution was founded on December 8, 1927, to merge the activities of the Institute for Government Research, founded in 1916, the Institute of Economics, founded in 1922, and the Robert Brookings Graduate School of Economics and Government, founded in 1924.

The Board of Trustees is responsible for the general administration of the Institution, while the immediate direction of the policies, program, and staff is vested in the President, assisted by an advisory committee of the officers and staff. The bylaws of the Institution state: "It is the function of the Trustees to make possible the conduct of scientific research, and publication, under the most favorable conditions, and to safeguard the independence of the research staff in the pursuit of their studies and in the publication of the results of such studies. It is not a part of their function to determine, control, or influence the conduct of particular investigations or the conclusions reached."

The President bears final responsibility for the decision to publish a manuscript as a Brookings book. In reaching his judgment on the competence, accuracy, and objectivity of each study, the President is advised by the director of the appropriate research program and weighs the views of a panel of expert outside readers who report to him in confidence on the quality of the work. Publication of a work signifies that it is deemed a competent treatment worthy of public consideration but does not imply endorsement of conclusions or recommendations.

The Institution maintains its position of neutrality on issues of public policy in order to safeguard the intellectual freedom of the staff. Hence interpretations or conclusions in Brookings publications should be understood to be solely those of the authors and should not be attributed to the Institution, to its trustees, officers, or other staff members, or to the organizations that support its research.

FOREWORD

In government and out, among sophisticated students of politics and casual observers of the political scene, in this country and abroad, belief in the virtual indestructibility of government organizations is entrenched. Many would say yes to the question asked in the title of this book.

But little systematic evidence supports such an answer. Somewhat more is known about the life span of private organizations; among them a short life is not unusual. Few of their governmental counterparts are assured of indefinite existence when they are created, but many of them seem methuselan if not everlasting. Yet the ensuing political and managerial difficulties would be staggering if it were true that old ones seldom die and new ones appear continually.

In this study, Herbert Kaufman, a Brookings senior fellow, brings together data bearing on the birth, longevity, and death of government organizations in an attempt to determine whether the common belief is valid. Treating his title as a question to be investigated empirically, rather than as a rhetorical flourish, he examined more than four hundred units of federal executive departments. His conclusions support the widespread impression that agencies stay alive once they have been born, but they also make clear that organizational death is not an unknown phenomenon. By showing that both births and deaths occur in spurts, this venture into unexplored territory demonstrates that such research can be of benefit to managerial practice and organization theory.

Many people in the federal bureaucracy cooperated with the author in this study; it is not possible to thank each of them individually here. On behalf of the author and the Brookings Institution, however, their contributions to the project are gratefully acknowledged. The editor of the manuscript, Elizabeth H. Cross, improved it substantively as well as stylistically, as did suggestions and criticisms by Gilbert Y. Steiner, Paul Quirk, and other readers. The author is grateful to Christine de Fontenay for her skillful and imaginative computer analysis of his data. Radmila Reinhart uncomplainingly typed and retyped it and kept track of the seemingly endless changes.

The views expressed in this study are the author's and should not be ascribed to the trustees, officers, or other staff members of the Brookings Institution.

KERMIT GORDON
President

February 1976
Washington, D.C.

CONTENTS

Tables

Figures

MAYBE YES, MAYBE NO

You frequently hear the opinion that government agencies hardly ever die—or fade away, either.[1] Once established, according to this view, they continue indefinitely, whether or not they are needed or useful or even wanted. They keep going because they enjoy some kind of natural immunity to the forces that kill off nongovernmental organizations.

If you stop to think about it, it's a startling idea. Even with an extremely low birth rate, a population of immortals would gradually attain immense proportions. Since it is known that the birth rate of government organizations is above zero, it follows that if they are immortal, public administration is headed for (or maybe even has arrived at) deep trouble.

Galvanizing administrative machinery made up of everlasting organizations would be a formidable task. Where time is unlimited, there is no sense of urgency; members of an organization assured of indefinite existence would probably be inclined to move at a much more leisurely pace than the rest of us can afford or tolerate. In their long view, matters pressing to most of us might well seem deferrable. Where we hold speedy decisions more important than carefully re-

1. For examples of published allegations of public-agency immortality, see James M. Beck, *Our Wonderland of Bureaucracy* (Macmillan, 1932), p. 67; Luther Gulick, "Notes on the Theory of Organization," in Luther Gulick and L. Urwick, eds., *Papers on the Science of Administration* (New York: Institute of Public Administration, 1937), p. 43; and Peter Drucker, *The Age of Discontinuity* (Harper and Row, 1968), p. 222. The opposite thesis—that government organizations survive only with great difficulty—is seldom advanced either orally or in print. A notable exception is Herbert A. Simon, Donald W. Smithburg, and Victor A. Thompson, *Public Administration* (Knopf, 1950), chaps. 18 and 19 and pp. 560–61. An even more extreme argument—that organizations in general tend to be short-lived—was put forth most emphatically by Chester I. Barnard in *The Functions of the Executive* (Harvard University Press, 1938), p. 5. But this seems to be a minority position, at least as far as public agencies are concerned.

For the most part, then, the mortality and longevity of public organizations are rarely studied and seldom discussed in the literature on public administration, and even writers' assumptions about them are hardly ever made explicit. The subject is largely neglected.

searched judgments, they would doubtless prefer painstaking study before taking any action. Choices that look critical to those of us whose mortality compels us to get on with things would appear trivial to an organization with an infinite time horizon.

Moreover, the incessant addition of organizations to the immortal band would surely multiply the interactions and "interfaces" in the system, increasing the number of clearances, reviews, and accommodations required for any action and augmenting the number of potential vetoes throughout the network. If the total volume of actions surviving this gamut were not reduced to a trickle, the decisiveness and vitality of the actions would be sapped and the cycle time for any individual decision lengthened intolerably.

Exerting political and managerial influence on such a system would present a staggering challenge. Political leaders attempting to change policies—that is, to alter what governmental administrative organizations do—and political administrators bent on improving coordination would find their nominal subordinates resistant to their direction because, to the people who internalize the perspective of their long-lived agencies, political figures are but birds of passage; agency personnel are likely to see themselves as the guardians of truly enduring values. In any case, since they will typically be around long after the politicians are gone, they will try to steer a steady course instead of swinging wildly in response to every "momentary" change in the wind.

Does all this sound like an indictment of today's administrative pathology rather than a portrait of some imaginary future bureaucratic inferno? No wonder, then, that many people have concluded the day of the immortal public organization is already upon us. And that even those who are skeptical of the cassandran prediction are nonetheless uneasy about the possible consequences of a constantly growing population of long-lived organizations (in the private as well as the public sphere) within the body politic.

Of course, it is conceivable that all these anxieties are groundless. If we simply let nature take its course, maybe the "parade of horribles" will never come to pass. It's hard to be complacent, however, when experience and intuition tell us we are in the early stages of a possibly serious disease. Still more worrisome is our lack of knowledge about the presumed ailment. Physicians who work with greater information and deeper understanding of their subject than do students of administration concede the dangers of doing more harm than good if they are not careful; iatrogenic (physician-induced) disorders are acknowledged. Shouldn't students of administration be at least as modest instead of leaping to conclusions about claimed deficiencies and prescribing remedies when we can be certain of so little?

We are certainly groping in the dark as far as organizational life patterns are concerned. We don't even know if the longevity of government organizations is, as alleged, rising. On the basis of impressions and deduction, this is certainly a plausible hypothesis. On the same basis, however, the opposite is equally plausible; there is as much reason to expect administrative agencies to be short-lived as long-lived. Look at the balance sheet.

FACTORS FAVORING LONG AGENCY LIFE

In the federal government, at least seven factors (or, more accurately, seven complexes of factors) do indeed tend to keep every agency born alive indefinitely.

1. For most of the history of the nation, administrative agencies were commonly established by statute or accorded statutory recognition. The distinction between the two is not trivial; if you go back over the record of the federal administrative structure, it is striking how many agencies were initially set in motion by action of a department head, later to acquire statutory underpinning by mention in an appropriations act, and only much later in their lifetime to be recognized in a piece of substantive legislation.[2] It is not clear in such cases whether the department head reached an understanding with the appropriate members of Congress before taking administrative action or seized the initiative because ratification of a fait accompli is easier to obtain than prior approval. Whatever the method and motives of statutory recognition, however, most government bureaus

2. For example, see Lloyd M. Short, *The Development of National Administrative Organization in the United States* (Johns Hopkins Press, 1923), pp. 225–27. Secretary Hamilton Fish reorganized the Department of State extensively in 1870 "acting under his general authority as head of the department." The chiefs of the bureaus he set up "were not recognized as such in the appropriation acts relating to the department, but were merely given that title by authority of the Secretary." Not until 1873 did Congress recognize the reorganization legislatively—in an appropriation act in March of that year.

for a long time enjoyed their own legislative base, and the various forms were, to all intents and purposes, equally secure.

A statutory base is for a number of reasons more secure than a departmental order or a presidential executive order even though it can obviously be altered or repealed by another statute. Enacting a significant piece of legislation in a representative body is a lengthy, tortuous process requiring extensive bargaining and trading to assemble a supporting majority; having achieved sufficient consensus to pass a bill, legislators are not ordinarily disposed to reverse themselves quickly. Moreover, the legislative process makes it easier to block action than to carry proposals to fruition; as James Sterling Young put it, a system designed to maximize representation is not necessarily well designed to govern.[3] Any legislation enacted becomes a vested interest of those who fought for it, and they will inevitably rise to its defense. The legislative setting tends to favor the defenders of the status quo—especially if the defenders have recently overcome the previous status quo to produce the current one.

Executive or administrative steps, by contrast, can be taken more readily. That is not to say the President and his department heads typically act unilaterally, without extensive consultation, negotiation, and agreement on important matters; executive and administrative decisions are organizational products rather than personal instruments in most cases.[4] But when they have the formal authority to resolve issues, executives are more frequently able to do so relatively quickly and emphatically than is a legislative body. That is why statutory underpinning is both sought and granted by those who want to confer a measure of security on their favorite administrative agencies, and why agencies buttressed by legislation can be expected to be more resistant to potentially lethal forces than their less fortunate counterparts.

Furthermore, when legislators have grappled with a problem and after long travail arrived at the best solution they can win consensus for, their attention shifts to all the other problems that crowd in on

3. *The Washington Community, 1800–1828* (Columbia University Press, 1966).

4. The term "organizational products" is from Paul H. Appleby, *Big Democracy* (Knopf, 1945), chaps. 8 and 9. See also David B. Truman, *The Governmental Process* (Knopf, 1951), chaps. 13 and 14; Robert A. Dahl, *Pluralist Democracy in the United States* (Rand McNally, 1967), pp. 325–29; Theodore C. Sorensen, *Decision-Making in the White House* (Columbia University Press, 1963).

them, and even those unhappy with the compromise are naturally reluctant to reopen the earlier controversy. That doesn't mean they never will. If an agency becomes a center of conflict and notoriety, it will rapidly move upward on the legislative agenda. In the ordinary course of events, however, legislators become preoccupied with other matters, and the new preoccupations make it probable that previously—especially recently—passed laws setting up agencies will not be rescinded or even substantially modified for a considerable period.

There was a time when turnover in Congress was high compared with what obtains today, which meant that many of the backers of agencies would not be around long to defend their creations. For generations, however, tenure in Congress has been growing more secure.[5] Sponsors are now likely to be on hand for a long while to protect the legislation they promoted.

It is therefore reasonable to infer that when a law appears on the books, it will remain there for a long time. An agency whose charter is embedded in statutes would seem to have a longer life expectancy than those set up by lesser instruments of creation.

2. Eventually, of course, the original sponsors and guardians of agencies disappear from Congress. That doesn't mean, though, that the agencies are thereupon left friendless and defenseless in the legislative chambers. Over time their legislative committees and subcommittees, their appropriations committees and subcommittees, and the committee staffs tend to develop possessive and protective attitudes toward them. Safe seats and the seniority system in Congress keep the same members of Congress in key posts for years on end, fostering cordial, comfortable personal relations with similarly entrenched leaders of administrative agencies. Committee clerks and senior staff likewise serve for long periods, developing friendly ties, mutual understandings, mutual appreciation, and mutual trust with the top managers of agencies within their jurisdiction. Sometimes it seems as though the command of some bureaus is shared between bureau chiefs and Capitol Hill.

Both sides benefit from the association. On its side, an agency gains shelter and security from critics and adversaries because most of the

5. Nelson W. Polsby, "The Institutionalization of the U.S. House of Representatives," *American Political Science Review*, vol. 62 (March 1968), pp. 145–48; H. Douglas Price, "The Congressional Career Then and Now," in Nelson W. Polsby, ed., *Congressional Behavior* (Random House, 1971), pp. 14–27.

business of Congress is conducted in committee; close association with the members and staff of the committees handling an agency's business with Congress is insurance against their using their great power in a damaging fashion, and also provides a sturdy shield against hostile forces. On the other side, members of Congress gain because a compliant agency augments their store of political currency—the ability to do favors for their general constituencies, for individual constituents, for their party supporters, and for their colleagues.

A cooperative agency, for example, may exercise its discretion about the location of facilities and about program emphases in such a way as to increase jobs, expenditures, and services in the states and districts of committee members, thereby enhancing the members' images at home. An agency may also take favorable and speedy action for clients on whose behalf strategically placed legislators intervene, thus earning for the legislators the gratitude and loyalty of those voters and political donors. And an agency may use its hiring power to the advantage of applicants recommended by powerful senators and representatives. Civil service laws, laws regulating contracting and purchasing decisions, the Administrative Procedure Act, and other legal provisions limit the extent of these practices, but it is impossible to make the laws so stringent as to eliminate agency discretion entirely.[6] Consequently, administrative discretion is often employed to the benefit of relevant elected officials.

This influence not only helps elected officials with the voters; by using it on behalf of other elected officers (who are then in their debt), they build a foundation to advance their own government careers, to increase their impact on substantive policy, and, by demands for reciprocity, to extend their capacity to do favors for claimants in areas outside their own jurisdiction.

So a congenial agency can do as much for the "right" members of Congress as the members of Congress can for the agency. And the "right" ones—the ranking members of committees—are those with great seniority, which means time has been working where it does the most good for an agency. Once the habit of cooperation and the network of reciprocal obligation become firmly established, the prospects for long agency life become bright indeed.

6. See Kenneth Culp Davis, *Administrative Law Treatise* (West, 1958), vol. 1, chap. 1; and Davis, *Discretionary Justice* (University of Illinois Press, 1971), chap. 1.

3. With or without powerful allies, federal agencies are the accidental beneficiaries of another fortuitously protective element: the size of the federal budget. The budget is now so huge that Congress and its subdivisions could not, even if they were inclined to, treat it as a totally new document each year. Rather, the record of expenditures in the recent past is taken as a base, and attention is focused on whether to exceed the base by some fraction (which is what agencies typically request), reduce it by some fraction (which is what agency critics and economy-minded people urge), or leave it as it is. Total elimination of funds for an established agency or even massive slashes approaching total elimination are unknown, for all practical purposes. In the jargon of the trade, budgets are normally incremental, not zero-base.

Consequently, once an agency receives appropriations, it is apt to be borne along by the sheer momentum of the budgetary process. The continuation of agency financing at a level fairly close to the level attained in the recent past is highly probable.[7] Whether the new congressional budget agency and new budgetary processes[8] will reduce the probability remains to be seen. Meanwhile, the degree of assurance against termination is quite high for any agency, thanks to the magnitude of federal expenditures.

In some ways, Congress has thus become a prisoner of its annual cycle. There is so much to review in so short a time that even extensive division of labor has not freed legislators to examine more than incremental adjustments. In any case, were more time available, reopening the entire budget of an agency every year would subject members of Congress to crushingly boring repetition; the same members, after all, sit in judgment on the same agencies year after year. While it is true the congressmen may thus become so well informed about the subjects under consideration that attention to budgetary changes is all that is necessary, it is also true that agencies can consequently approach their overseers confident that most of their financial foundation will not be questioned. If Congress ever lengthens its budgetary perspectives, the situation may change substantially. Until then, the realities of budgeting provide most agencies with a reassuringly snug harbor.

7. Aaron Wildavsky, *The Politics of the Budgetary Process* (Little, Brown, 1964), pp. 125, 150–51.

8. Described briefly in *Congressional Quarterly Weekly Report*, vol. 32 (June 15, 1974), pp. 1590–94.

4. Some agencies are further sheltered by their comparative invulnerability to departmental and even presidential control. This observation applies not only to more than fifty "independent" organizations deliberately insulated from such influence, including such giants as the Postal Service, the Veterans Administration, and the General Services Administration, as well as the regulatory commissions, but also to some bureaus ostensibly within the executive departments. Cabinet officers and the President himself have occasionally lamented their impotence in dealing with some nominal subordinates, the Army Corps of Engineers and the Federal Bureau of Investigation at times being extreme but instructive examples.

Immunity to executive supervision increases agency durability by insulating administration from the disposition of executives to "rationalize" it. Presumably, executives have stronger incentives to do so because they are more concerned with efficiency than their congressional brethren, who are theoretically better able to get favors from a fragmented system than they could from a neatly ordered one in which nonelected officials were dominant. Moreover, a fragmented system allegedly imposes more demands on scarce executive time than a "streamlined" system, so executives are always trying to reorganize in order to escape avalanches of detail and thereby free themselves for the formulation of "broad policies." At bottom, however, one suspects the real reason for executives' enthusiasm for changing administrative structure is their determination to gain control of the machinery of governmental administration. By terminating or dismembering old organizations and creating new ones, they evidently hope to assert their command of the execution of policy pronouncements.

But cabinet and subcabinet officers stay in office for comparatively short periods, and even the presidency turns over frequently from the viewpoint of an agency and its allies in Congress and outside the government.[9] Time is therefore on the agencies' side; their superiors are gone before many changes can be formulated or implemented, so

9. The "typical" high-level, federal civil servant has had twenty-three years of continuous federal service, mostly in one or two occupational fields and one or two departments or agencies; David T. Stanely, *The Higher Civil Service* (Brookings Institution, 1964), pp. 22–27. Political executives, on the other hand, served in their positions an average of two to three years; David T. Stanely, Dean E. Mann, James W. Doig, *Men Who Govern* (Brookings Institution, 1967), chap. 4, especially pp. 56–61.

merely delaying action is tantamount to stopping it. Moreover, their expertise in their specialties makes outsiders, including superiors, who are comparative amateurs, hesistant to intervene lest they do real damage and open themselves to charges of political interference. The bureaus are shielded by circumstance from their nominal over-lords, and while not totally proof against death from this cause, they are in practice quite secure.

5. Agencies do not rely exclusively on circumstance, however. They are not helpless, passive pawns in the game of politics as it affects their lives; they are active, energetic, persistent participants. The motives of their leaders and members to preserve the organizations to which they belong are very strong. The techniques they can use are abundant, and their experience in using them is extensive.

One of their strongest motives is job preservation. For many, the continuation of an agency makes the difference between having a job and being unemployed for a time; they will naturally be especially defensive. But even those who can be reasonably sure of continued employment elsewhere have vested interests in their settled and secure ways, their established seniority, their place in the scheme of things, their functional routines. The preference for the familiar and the predictable over the unknown is widespread. All of this can be jeopardized if prevailing arrangements are upset. Most organization members will therefore join the battle for agency survival.

For the leaders, the incentives are even greater. Their reputations are tied to their agencies, and the fate of their organizations may profoundly affect their professional status and perhaps even their employability in government and out. They are particularly resistant to the dismemberment of their structures.

Strong as the material motives are, however, they are probably matched by the mysterious forces of organizational loyalty and commitment to program, which are perhaps the most powerful of organizational bonds. Nationalism is a particularly intense form of organizational loyalty rarely approached in other types of organizations, yet if an organization were united by only a fraction of the same magnetism, it would hold together under the most trying circumstances. Not all organizations develop such unity. But any government agency with a history behind it, a record of achievement to its credit, and a corps of officers and employees who have been with it for some time is likely to exhibit some of it. Consequently, when the agency's existence is threatened, its people rally around it in ways sometimes surprising even to themselves.

Once aroused, they have a large arsenal of weapons to employ in their agencies' defense.[10] They cultivate their allies and the mass media. Covertly and openly, they attack and try to embarrass their adversaries. They strike bargains to appease the foes they cannot overcome. If this sounds like warfare, it is—at least a type of warfare, a struggle for organizational existence. Organizations engage in it all the time, but with particular intensity when those who are part of them perceive their organizations' very lives as threatened.

6. They also have friends outside the government who look after them. Their clienteles are commonly among their most ardent defenders.

Such a cordial association between a service agency and the people it serves is hardly surprising; one expects no less. That it should characterize the relationship between *regulatory* agencies and the interests they *control* is less obvious; one might more reasonably anticipate hostility in this case. Nevertheless, those who are regulated are often as solicitous of their regulators as those served are of their benefactors.

The reason is that many regulated interests benefit greatly from control. To be sure, control tends to impose a ceiling on their profits. But at the same time it tends to shield them from unfettered competition—by restricting entry into the regulated marketplace, by prohibiting destructive practices, and other means. A truly competitive marketplace is absolutely ruthless; regulators can be induced to show mercy. Indeed, it is now recognized that regulatory bodies gradually come to identify with the people they oversee, turning into guardians of their perceptions and values.[11] Ultimately, the thought of life without the regulators becomes terrifying to the regulated.

10. See, for example, Morton H. Halperin, *Bureaucratic Politics and Foreign Policy* (Brookings Institution, 1974), chaps. 6–14; Wallace S. Sayre and Herbert Kaufman, *Governing New York City* (Norton, 1965), pp. 251–63, 352–57. Although the examples in the latter book are drawn from experience in New York City government, the general strategies are applicable to the federal setting.

11. Marver H. Bernstein, *Regulating Business by Independent Commission* (Princeton University Press, 1955), pp. 154–60, 295; William O. Douglas, *Go East, Young Man* (Random House, 1974), p. 294.

So whether an agency provides services for its clients or regulates them, its clientele can frequently be counted on to come to its assistance when it is in trouble. At the very least, even if its clients are critical of the agency, they may oppose efforts to terminate it; it is a known quantity, and who can tell what, if anything, might replace it if it were allowed to go down? Automatically, therefore, a beleaguered agency will ordinarily be joined in its struggles by its clients.

7. Another set of external allies is the professional or trade association with which the dominant occupational group to be found in almost every bureau is identified. Doctors, lawyers, engineers, accountants, bankers, geologists, veterinaries, social workers, foresters, nurses, economists, teachers, craftsmen, letter carriers, professional soldiers, police chiefs, and many other specialists are particularly influential in one agency or another. All of them have organizations that both watch over occupational standards and represent the occupations as interest groups. When "their" respective agencies are menaced, they mobilize to defend them.

In part, their interest is symbolic; there is status in an occupation that is virtually the exclusive path of entry to leadership of a significant section of officialdom. In part, their interest is public-spirited; they are genuinely concerned that only qualified practitioners of their arts be admitted to practice. In part, their interest is practical; as long as positions are restricted to them, or even as long as their trade is favored in the competition for appointment, a significant block of public jobs is assured for them. The attractiveness of a trade, the drawing power of its trade schools, and the treasury of its association or union may be enhanced by these opportunities it seems to control. Finally, the interest of the trades is political; occupying strategic places inside the government is presumed to give them a more effective voice in the formation of policies that impinge on them and to provide advance information on what is happening that might affect them.

So when the existence of an agency is endangered, such associations become another factor in the outcome. They greatly increase the probability that it will not succumb.

When all seven of the foregoing factors are taken together, the contention that government agencies are virtually immortal seems incontestable.

HAZARDS TO AGENCY SURVIVAL

On the other hand, when you reflect on the number, variety, and virulence of the perils to which agencies are inescapably exposed, you may begin to wonder that any of them survive for any time at all.

1. The same factors that buffer a government organization against potentially lethal forces also limit its ability to respond to changes in its environment. If the relevant environment of government organizations were constant, with changes occurring so slowly that the response capabilities of agencies, no matter how circumscribed, were never severely taxed, inflexibility would make no difference. Almost certainly, there must be at least corners and crannies where this is the case. I take it to be axiomatic, however, that a static state in the federal administrative establishment is an exception and that ceaseless, restless, sometimes furious ferment is the rule.[12] Under such conditions, an organization fixed in its ways would have a difficult time.

Many government agencies are rendered nearly immobile by their protective armor. For example, the near permanence of the statutes that created many agencies can restrict their freedom of action. As the circumstances that gave rise to the agencies give way to new circumstances and as experience in administering programs suggests new ways of doing things, new legislation will often be required to permit needed organizational or program or geographic changes. But the legislative process is a tortuous obstacle course; bills often move through it very slowly. The grants of authority that gave life to administrative organizations can turn into prisons for the organizations because they do not easily keep up with the times.

Out-of-date enabling acts are likely to result in poorer agency performance; rusty tools do not make for superior work. Although the fault may not lie with the agency, it is the visible executor and there-

12. The axiom is a large assumption—there are no widely accepted indicators of environmental stability, so the axiom rests entirely on personal impressions. Obviously, if the approach employed in this study is to prove fruitful, more objective indicators will have to be developed. Fortunately, work is proceeding in this direction; see Raymond E. Miles, Charles C. Snow, and Jeffrey Pfeffer, "Organization-Environment: Concepts and Issues," *Industrial Relations*, vol. 13 (October 1974), pp. 244–64, especially the discussion and the literature cited on pp. 247–50.

fore the inevitable lightning rod. As the quality and quantity of out-put fall, as the relevance of the agency's activities to the problems at hand grows more tenuous, or as the backlog of problems increases, it is generally on the agency that the blame falls. Its erstwhile sup-porters begin to defect, its appropriations decrease, and its capacity to perform is thereby curtailed still further. It may slide into mortal trouble through no fault of its own.

Nor are statutes the only, or even the chief, cause of inadapt-ability. An agency's friends and allies also contribute to its inflexi-bility. For their support comes at a price—the right to be consulted and to interdict any action that might affect them. In recent times, some commentators on the political scene have applauded the demo-cratic qualities of such participation. But there is no denying that it complicates and slows action. Any bureau chief who has tried to close a branch office can testify to these difficulties. Most bureau chiefs can also bear witness to the groundwork that must be done to prepare the way for changes of policy, or even of emphasis within the framework of long-standing policies, if members of a coalition are not to be alienated; expectations of veto rights form quickly and precipi-tate bitter resentment if they are disappointed. That is one reason agency leaders move cautiously, with short, tentative steps, much of the time. Their hesitancy, in turn, slows agency reaction to a world in flux, which would seem logically to set the scene for a high death rate.

Many other factors, such as habit, the temptations of the familiar and safe path, the processes of socialization that produce conformity, and capital investments, also limit organizational adaptability; these have been described elsewhere.[13] What is of special interest here is the double-edged character of the factors that seemingly sustain an agency against life-shortening troubles. Even they can contribute to its demise.

2. The portrait of government agencies as removed from competi-tion and its often fatal effects is greatly oversimplified. There are doubtless a number of certifiable monopolies, but far more agencies must meet the challenge of rivals inside the machinery of government standing ready to take over their functions—and perhaps engaged in deliberate campaigns to do so. Although the organizational ideal of

13. Herbert Kaufman, *The Limits of Organizational Change* (University of Alabama Press, 1971), chaps. 1, 3.

many management analysts is an administrative structure free of
ambiguities of mission, jurisdiction, and authority, and although in-
termittent progress has been made toward that ideal since the President's Committee on Administrative Management decried the un-
planned character of the federal administrative establishment,[14]
"overlapping" and "duplication"—the familiar twin bogeymen of
efficiency experts—still flourish in the government. The government
remains a patchwork in many ways.

Given the general fragmentation of American society, political
parties, and Congress itself, things could hardly be otherwise. In addition, specific tactical considerations conduce to administrative
fragmentation. For example, the sponsors of new programs prefer to
lodge their brainchildren in new organizations that will give them
undivided attention rather than in old agencies in which the new
responsibilities will be added to a long list of preexisting duties.
Sometimes congressmen choose agency location because they fear
that the dictates of administrative symmetry and functional consis-
tency will place important programs under officials they disagree
with: the Reconstruction Finance Corporation, for example, was
taken out of the Department of Commerce to remove it from the authority of Secretary Henry A. Wallace, whose standing with Congress was low; and the Economic Cooperation Administration (the
original foreign aid agency) was made autonomous and its admin-
istrator given status equal to the heads of executive departments because of congressional determination to prevent its domination by a
State Department then in bad odor with the legislative majority.
Sometimes competing agencies are for this reason deliberately set up

14. *Report: Administrative Management in the Government of the United States*
(Government Printing Office, 1937). "The Executive Branch of the Government
of the United States," the committee observed (p. 32), "has thus grown up without plan or design like the barns, shacks, silos, tool sheds, and garages of an old
farm. . . . Owing to the multiplicity of agencies and the lack of administrative
management, there is waste, overlapping, and duplication which may be eliminated through coordination, consolidation, and proper managerial control."
But the committee recognized this formulation as an ideal, not a practical objective. "Government," they said (pp. 37–38), "is a going concern, not a static
institution. . . . While this does not change the principles of organization, it does
alter profoundly their application in individual cases. . . . It must be remembered that no organization of so complicated a nature and endowed with so
many traditions as the Federal Government can be strictly logical."

to perform functions already being performed by an ongoing agency; the Tennessee Valley Authority had its own agricultural, forestry, recreational, and other services in addition to its power dams, and the Department of Agriculture, the Department of the Interior, and the Corps of Engineers joined hands to prevent similar "intrusions" into their jurisdictions in the Missouri Valley.[15] Clashes are also provoked inadvertently by vague legislative drafting, incomplete legislative information about existing organizations and their functions, or sheer administrative imperialism on the part of an aggressive leader. Every so often, heroic attempts to rationalize the system are undertaken, and occasionally they are impressively (though never totally) successful. But the creation and scattering of new organizations go on constantly. Symmetry and orderliness do not last long.

That is why almost any agency will probably perceive at least one other agency as a direct competitor. Usually, the two arrive at some understanding and divide the field (or have it divided for them) so as not to engage in incessant warfare. On the other hand, each of them is aware that another organization in operation has the ability to take over its own job. Some of these situations are well known; the Bureau of Reclamation and the Corps of Engineers, for instance, have many similar capacities, and components of the Departments of the Interior and of Agriculture are equally involved in natural resource protection, development, and management. Other overlaps are probably less obvious. There is tension, for instance, between the Bureau of Customs and the Immigration and Naturalization Service over smugglers on the Mexican border.[16] Client-oriented bureaus such as the Bureau of Indian Affairs and the Veterans Administration do some of the same things as more general health, welfare, and education agencies. Both the Antitrust Division of the Justice Department and the Federal Trade Commission have some responsibility for the maintenance of economic competition in the business sector. The general counsel of several departments and agencies would like to break the Justice Department's monopoly on representation of the government in court.[17]

15. Martha Derthick, *Between State and Nation* (Brookings Institution, 1974), pp. 42–43.

16. An open battle erupted into the pages of *The New York Times* of July 3, 1974.

17. Donald L. Horowitz, "The Jurocracy" (in manuscript), chap. 6.

The list could be extended almost indefinitely, but there is no need to labor the point. If the existence of competitors able and ready to take over the functions of every organization disciplines the organizations by threatening their lives, the federal administrative environment is by no means as benign as some people paint it.

3. In fact, even agencies in wholly dissimilar kinds of work are in competition with one another. The federal treasury is not bottomless and they all draw from it. Some therefore gain at the expense of others. When federal revenues increase rapidly, the conflicts are minimized. When they do not, the conflicts can grow very sharp. The demands of the military as against those of civilian bureaus, of foreign economic assistance vis-à-vis domestic requirements, of city-oriented agencies versus agricultural and rural agencies, for example, are exceedingly divisive at times. The image of government organizations tranquilly and securely going through their routines is at variance with reality much of the time.

Conflicts of this sort, of course, are almost never fatal by themselves. The competition is over shares of the pie, not for all of the pie or none. But it is important to remember that the ability of a government organization to do favors for its friends and allies and to administer its programs effectively depends in large measure on the trends in its budget. Hence, when it starts to lose out financially, there is a good chance other life-sustaining capabilities will also decline. Although such a downward spiral would clearly take considerable time to reach a lethal level, it is still a disquieting development to the members and leaders of an agency. Death from indirect competition may come slowly, but it is death nonetheless.

4. But organizations may also decline and disappear when there are no competitors depriving them of sustenance. The circumstances of their birth alone may doom them.

For example, it is not unheard of to set up organizations for the purpose of creating positions with which to compensate distinguished public service or simply to reward friends. Sometimes the objective is even to provide a nonhumiliating place of exile for an enemy or an incompetent too strongly entrenched to dismiss or demote. Organizations with such origins are apt to experience difficulty building constituencies in Congress and in the public, so their existence is unlikely to continue beyond the tenure of the intended beneficiary.

Sometimes units are established to provide services for which a demand is only imagined or momentary. When the absence of a market for their output is perceived, the discovery will usually result in their termination (though it is surprising how long they can continue when there is nothing for them to do).

Agencies are also set up as symbolic responses to real problems. The sponsors may have nothing more in mind than projecting a false image of vigorous action to quiet a growing clamor.[18] Or they may hope the agencies will find feasible solutions that have hitherto eluded the sponsors. Such gestures can generate false hope, deep disappointment, and eventually bitter resentment. Indeed, unrealistic expectations about what an agency can achieve may bring it down even when its creation is not a deceptive maneuver; excessively high hopes may prove fatal whether the agency intentionally fostered them or not.

So some agencies are brought into the world under conditions that practically guarantee their life will be limited. Even without direct competitors, their future may be bleak.

Furthermore, they expire because they make mistakes or become the victims of mistakes. Let them be cautious when they ought to be firm, forceful when conciliation is required, accommodating when they ought to be defending basic principles, or unyielding when flexibility would save the day, and they may end up losing their effectiveness and their reputations--and ultimately their identities. Let the agencies themselves, governmental staff agencies, or appropriations committees, or all three, underestimate the financial or personnel or matériel needs of the job to be done, and the shortages may reduce performance to levels that destroy confidence in and support for them.

The struggle for survival, in short, is not only a struggle against other organizations competing directly or indirectly for the things they all need. The environment itself can kill them off.

5. Every agency has natural enemies as well as natural allies. The more conscientiously it does its job, the more surely it will rouse critics and adversaries who are always looking for opportunities to deliver a blow. Yet if an agency attempts to avoid rousing them by generosity in the form of excessive accommodation of their demands,

18. See Murray Edelman, *The Symbolic Uses of Politics* (University of Illinois Press, 1964).

it may drive its supporters into the opposition camp. Agencies thus walk a tightrope and sometimes find anything they do sets off storms of controversy from the most unexpected as well as the most predictable quarters.

This dilemma confronts agencies regardless of function. Welfare bureaus, for example, will enjoy the backing of their clientele if they are lenient in the administration of vexatious rules, but they will come under the fire of other groups denouncing toleration of "freeloading" or ineligibility. If the bureaus try to appease such groups, the clients turn on them for their excessive bureaucratic defensiveness and the inequities and hardship they inflict on the intended beneficiaries of compassionate legislation. And if the bureaus try to compromise, they are as likely to cause discontent on both sides of the fence as to satisfy both.

A regulatory body is in a similar situation. If it insists the affected industries provide high-quality products, maximum occupational safety for their employees, and low prices for consumers, the regulated interests will mobilize against it. If it is sympathetic to the regulated interests, the adversely affected consumers or workers and their friends will take up cudgels against it. If it therefore decides to swing back to strict administration, production may drop—if not at once, at least in the future as capital investment falls off and fails to keep pace with the demands of a rising population. Consumers and employees will not like that, either, and will join the producers' attacks on the agency; that the motives of the several sets of critics are irreconcilably at odds with each other will not necessarily diminish the effectiveness of their joint assault.

As in the case of the other hazards to agency existence, such opposition or criticism does not by itself result in the death of agencies, at least in the short run. But when you think of the quicksand around which government organizations must make their way, their lives look less and less secure.

6. The normal oscillations of power between the parties and among factions within the parties are yet another potential quicksand. It stands to reason that the proud organizational instruments of one administration will loom in the eyes of the victors as tools of, and monuments to, the predecessors just vanquished at the polls; for years, social security was a lightning rod of this kind, and though its critics discovered it was too popular and socially useful to discard

when they finally came to office, the open and announced hostility of a political party sure to be elevated to power sooner or later certainly could not have enhanced the agency's sense of well-being and confidence about its future. At least in the early years of an agency's life, the chance that it will be regarded as a captive of its creators may be great enough to cast a shadow on its continuation even if the incoming party endorses the program it administers; the program, after all, can be reassigned to a more congenial organization.

Anxiety about this possibility and the discontinuities it might introduce into public administration and into the nation's social and economic life led to some of the familiar reforms designed to keep partisan politics out of administration. Without stability, long-range planning and investment would cease and national development would grind slowly to a stop. That is why so many parts of the government were given firm statutory underpinnings, why important functions were entrusted to independent commissions and public corporations outside the normal executive hierarchy, and why civil service and other procedural safeguards were placed about positions up to the highest levels of the administrative edifice. These measures fortify agencies against the effects of party turnover, including partisan efforts to replace existing agencies.

Logically, however, it could be reasoned that they intensify the hazards to existing agencies instead of diminishing them. In the days when a new administration could replace the leadership of government bureaus soon after taking office, the incentives to dismantle the bureaus were minimal; the bureaus could be brought into policy alignment by appropriate staffing. Indeed, that was one of the justifications advanced on behalf of the spoils system. When, on the other hand, a new administration finds itself confronting organizations manned by comparatively permanent corps of personnel, the temptation to do away with them and set up new, more compliant ones must occasionally seem almost irresistible, especially after the other party has been in power for a long time. Democratic government, after all, presumes obedience to elected officials on the part of administrative personnel at all subordinate levels, and it is not unreasonable to expect more cheerful and prompt obedience from people sympathetic to the current administration than from people opposed to its platform. If you couldn't restaff agencies, wouldn't you abolish them and establish new ones more likely to be loyal?

Things are not that simple. In the first place, flagrant violation of the popular ideal of the civil service—one free of partisan ties—might kindle widespread outrage. Second, while agencies engage in political strategies in defense of their existence and their programs, they usually avoid total identification with either party—for the very reason that intimate ties of this sort could well be their undoing. That is, compliance with the directives of the party in power is both a moral obligation and a life-preserving tactic. And finally, it is not a simple thing to destroy an ongoing agency; the sustaining forces are something to reckon with, and the increment of additional obedience obtained by destruction will not always be worth the expenditure of political capital it entails. So the incentives for an incoming administration to strike out with a meat ax at all existing agencies are sharply checked.

Consequently, change of parties does not necessarily produce a massive wave of administrative fatalities. Inevitably, however, at least some agencies—especially those closely linked to the outgoing administration—feel the chill wind of uncertainty. The risks may be moderate, but they are great enough to inflict more than a few casualties.

7. If all the foregoing were not enough to cast doubt on organizational immortality in the executive branch, the recent erosion of one of the bases of agency security—statutory underpinning—must certainly crack the stereotype. For a quarter of a century, in response to the recommendations of the first Hoover Commission,[19] heads of the major departments have been invested with broad discretion over the structure of their institutions. The logic of protection by legislation has not withered, but it has been challenged by the competing imperatives of greater managerial flexibility for the purposes of efficiency and adaptation to changing times. A series of reorganization plans in 1950 transferred to the secretaries all the functions of their

19. U.S. Commission on Organization of the Executive Branch of the Government, *General Management of the Executive Branch* (GPO, 1949), Recommendation 20 (p. 41): "We recommend that the department head be given authority to determine the organization within his department. He should be given authority to assign funds appropriated by the Congress for a given purpose to that agency in his department which he believes can best effect the will of Congress." See also the commission's *Task Force Report on Departmental Management* (GPO, 1949), pp. 6–8, and Joseph P. Harris, *Congressional Control of Administration* (Brookings Institution, 1964), pp. 19–25, 42–44.

subordinate officers, employees, and agencies; authorized the secretaries to redelegate those functions at will; and permitted them to freely transfer records, property, personnel, and funds within their departments.[20] The long-standing insulation of the bureaus from the power of their department heads was thus decisively breached.

The secretaries of some departments have not been hesitant to employ the authority given them in this fashion. In Commerce, Health, Education, and Welfare, Housing and Urban Development, Labor, and Agriculture, for example, units have been extensively combined, shifted, or given new assignments. Some, such as the Social and Rehabilitation Service, were even created by secretarial action.

Very real limits still circumscribe the discretion of department heads. Legally as well as politically, they cannot do everything they might want. But they are much stronger than they were before the new provisions were adopted in 1950, and structural modifications of the departments now occur as a matter of course.

To the agencies in the departments, the discretion of the secretaries presents yet another exposure to potentially threatening forces. The agencies may take some comfort in the knowledge that they are not utterly helpless before this hazard, but they can hardly dismiss the unpleasant fact that their organizational identity is far less secure than it once was.

One might infer that the combined weight of all seven sets of hazards afflicting government organizations would lead to a substantial death rate among them. Far from enjoying an almost certain prospect of indefinite existence, they seem likely to share the outlook of the combat soldier: abstractly, the odds of surviving are in his favor, but the casualty rate in the front lines is too high to justify complacency, and the longer he remains there, the greater is his fear of suffering severe injury from one of the dangers. If there were only a single threat, the menace would still be depressing; when there are many, the prospects are downright discouraging; and when several, or even all of them, can occur simultaneously, the future must be frightening to contemplate.

20. See Appendix, Title 5, United States Code, for the 1950 (and 1953) reorganization plans effecting this change. For a specific illustration, note Reorganization Plan 3 of 1958, secs. 1, 2, 5.

A LOGICAL DILEMMA

The deductive case for a large mortality rate among government organizations thus appears approximately as plausible as the deductive
case for their immortality. But deciding that one argument is logically stronger than the other would not establish the validity of such
a conclusion; a better-reasoned argument is not necessarily a more
accurate description. Abstract reasoning will not answer the question
posed in the title of this book.

Neither will anecdotal evidence. On the one hand, there are organizations with a record of corporate existence and continuous operation from 1789 to the present (such as the Departments of State and
of the Treasury). On the other, it is not difficult to identify organizations that did not last as long as a dozen years (such as the National
Youth Administration, the Civilian Conservation Corps, and the
Works Progress Administration of New Deal days).

To find out which argument is more nearly right requires a more
systematic review of experience than that. That is what this study
sets out to provide.

THE QUEST FOR AN ANSWER

Probably the best way to answer the question that inspired this research would be to compile lists of federal agencies in existence every year for an extended period and compare the lists to see how many endured for the whole interval, how many died, how many were born, what changes took place in the average age of the organizational population, and what the trends in agency longevity were.

Because the data are not easy to come by, such a compilation would be a monumental undertaking. Even if one avoided the complications of trying to reconstruct the lists for the past and began the data collection with the current year and carried it forward for many years, being content to reap the harvest in the distant future, the required investment of time and money would hardly be justified without some prior indications that the project had promise of yielding the answers sought.

This study, then, is a search for these indications. On a scale much more modest than the ideal inquiry would require, it is a pilot investigation, not a definitive answer to the motivating question. It compares lists of federal agencies in 1923 and 1973; the limitations of time and funds would not cover additional readings. It includes some data on agency births, deaths, longevity, survival, and average organizational age. In addition, it describes trends in line-staff proportions and in the changing legal instruments of creation.

THE DATA

The lists of organizations surveyed were confined, for purposes of manageability, to ten of the eleven executive departments in existence in 1973 and the Executive Office of the President. The Department of Defense is so massive, and probably so atypical, that data from it would have overwhelmed the data from the others as well as absorbing a disproportionate share of the available research resources. Also excluded was the U.S. Postal Service, which was an executive department in 1923 but was transformed into an independent establishment in 1971; its size, like that of the Defense Depart-

23

ment, presented formidable difficulties, and its recent transformation was accompanied by extensive internal reorganization greatly complicating the problem of fitting it in with the other subjects on the specimen tray. More than fifty agencies commonly treated as "independent"—which is to say outside the executive departments and therefore less directly under presidential supervision—and scores of special boards, committees, and commissions were not covered, as this seemed impractical; while the executive departments and their components are probably no less diverse a collection of organizations than these, at least the departments have a common designation in the governmental structure and together make up a defensible as well as a workable selection.

The universe of organizations studied was further narrowed by omitting field offices. Attention was concentrated on departmental headquarters units and on the major subdivisions of the departments —essentially, bureaus and groups of bureaus. The components of the latter units were excluded even though some of them are exceedingly large, older than the departments of which they are part, and as complex internally as any organizations in the population analyzed.

Despite all these exclusions, the total number of organizations remaining in the universe is 421. They are an exceedingly mixed group in size, function, history, and budget; indeed, any such aggregation of federal organizations is likely to be much more varied in all these respects than a corresponding number of firms in a given industry. That is why they are such fascinating, as well as frustrating, objects of organizational studies; attributes common to most of them must be common to many types of organizations because they are already common to such a diverse group.

Nevertheless, it is important to bear in mind that the 421 organizations covered in this analysis are not the whole of federal governmental administration, and they are certainly not representative of the larger world of organizations. This study, with its restricted compass and only two soundings, is a hesitant and very short first step, a testing of the water. It is illustrative, not probative.

RESEARCH PROBLEMS

No less vexing than reducing the number of organizations to manageable size was the difficulty of determining the dates of birth and death of agencies. For organizations, birth and death, and therefore longevity, are elusive concepts.

Consider a specific case. On November 3, 1961, State Department Delegation of Authority 104 established the Agency for International Development as an agency within the department. (This action was directed and authorized by presidential Executive Order 10973 of the same date. The President, in turn, had been given authority over assistance programs by the Foreign Assistance Act of 1961, which also conferred on him the power to exercise his authority through whatever agency he chose.) On the surface, the date of birth seems unequivocal.

But the Agency for International Development consisted of essentially the same people who had constituted the International Cooperation Administration, which was abolished by the Foreign Assistance Act of 1961. What is more, they were located in the same places they had been in and were doing the same things they had been doing. In any ordinary sense, the AID would seem to have been the old ICA in a different guise. Thus the AID was really "born" as an organization before it was legally redesignated; its origin goes back at least as far as the birth of the ICA.

Why did the government go through this ritual when the organization remained, at least for the time, virtually intact? Apparently, the intent was to reduce the independence of the foreign assistance agency, which up to then had enjoyed semiautonomous status in the State Department. The change emphasized the subordination of foreign assistance administration to the President and, by his direction, the secretary of state, and also enabled them, at their discretion, to make further administrative changes. By ceremonially terminating the old agency and proclaiming the creation of a new one, all ambiguities about the relation of foreign assistance administration to the President and the State Department were eliminated. But the continuity between the ICA and the AID was not interrupted.

The ICA, in its turn, was a reincarnation of the Foreign Operations Administration. Acting under the provisions of the Mutual Security Act of 1954, the President in 1955 issued Executive Order 10610, which abolished the FOA and transferred its military aid functions to the Defense Department and its nonmilitary functions to the State Department. By State Department Delegation of Authority 85 of June 30, 1955, the secretary of state set up the ICA as a semiautonomous agency in his department. In this way, what had previously been classified as an independent agency (instead of as a component of an executive department) was brought part of the way back into the fold.

The FOA had been set up by Reorganization Plan 7 of 1953, which assembled in one agency the functions of the Mutual Security Agency, the Technical Cooperation Administration, and a number of other foreign-aid programs. The Mutual Security Agency owed its existence to the Mutual Security Act of 1951, which gave it the functions of the Economic Cooperation Administration (the original Marshall Plan agency) established by the Economic Cooperation Act of 1948, and which abolished the ECA.

Each of these transitions could justifiably be treated as the death of one organization and the birth of another. After all, official birth and death certificates attest the events. I nevertheless elected to treat this whole sequence of organizations as transformations in the life of a single, ongoing body. It seemed to me to parallel the stages in the development of a moth; despite radical differences in structure and behavior, larva, pupa, and imago are regarded as phases in the career of a single individual. So too are many abrupt changes in the form and character of organizations.

One reason for this decision was my determination to counteract my incentives to discover that organizations in the federal government have much shorter lives and that the turnover among them is much higher than conventional belief holds. This inquiry having been impelled by doubts about the validity of the common assumption that they almost never die, it stands to reason that I would unconsciously tend to confirm my basic premise—so as to vindicate the project and also to enjoy the ego gratification and the attention that come from challenging orthodoxy instead of verifying it. I was obliged to bend over backwards to promote objectivity.

In any case, it makes little sense to construe every name change, legal technicality, and tactical manipulation as an equivalent of organizational birth or death. As the metamorphoses of the foreign assistance agencies demonstrate, organizational adjustments may be more symbolic than substantive. A pronouncement of death may be issued to signal an attitude or shed an unfavorable image or even to terminate legal liabilities (as in the case of bankruptcy in the private sector) rather than to recognize the true demise of an agency. Similarly, a birth announcement may be an attempt to wipe clean the slate for a continuing organization rather than to celebrate the appearance of a new arrival. Indeed, some agencies have been officially abolished and nominally replaced by successors apparently for the purpose of ousting an officer who would otherwise be politically or legally immune to dismissal. Maneuvers of these kinds are sufficiently familiar to dissuade one from taking every public declaration of agency birth and death at face value.

That is why the Agency for International Development is, in this study, regarded as having been born in 1948, and why the Federal Highway Administration, established formally in 1966, is traced back to its origin in the Department of Agriculture's Office of Road Inquiry, set up in 1893. Scores of judgments of this kind were made in the course of assembling the data. I would be the first to admit that reasonable persons might differ over every choice. The bias, however, is heavily in favor of continuity, thus offsetting the inducements to exaggerate turnover.

The decision to trace existing agencies through their antecedents in identifying births and deaths instead of merely accepting documents without question forced me to adopt some rough indicators of organizational death. After all, organizations constantly make all sorts of marginal adjustments to their fluid internal and external environments. How many changes must occur, of what magnitude, and over what stretch of time before we say they have expired?[1]

This problem is not confined to public agencies; it applies to all organizations. Take the case of a manufacturing company. If it changed its name and nothing else, nobody would contend it had ceased to exist. If it also changed its product—maybe even if it replaced its top officers—it would probably still be perceived as the same firm. But what if it also changed its rank-and-file membership? Its clientele? Its location? Its structure? Its owners? Its creditors and debtors?

There is not nearly as much ambiguity about the death of a per-

1. The discussion of organizational death is taken from Herbert Kaufman, *The Limits of Organizational Change* (University of Alabama Press, 1971), pp. 114–18. See also President's Committee on Administrative Management, *Report: Administrative Management in the Government of the United States* (GPO, 1937), p. 37: "There is among governmental agencies great need for a coroner to pronounce them dead and for an undertaker to dispose of the remains."

son. If a man should change his name, ply a new trade, migrate to a new country, lose his hair, grow a beard, double his weight, take a new wife, acquire a new language, experience dramatic personality changes, and lose his memory, he would still be considered the same human being. Some uncertainties remain about the precise moment at which human life begins or terminates, imposed by abortion controversies and the development of organ transplants, but the range of difference, though it generates intense passion, is not terribly broad.

Human death is comparatively easily identified because it is defined by only a few discontinuities. When heartbeat stops for a length of time, blood pressure falls to zero, and electrochemical activity in the central nervous system disappears, no other continuities matter; the person is dead. If these processes go on, the person is called "alive" no matter what else changes.

Are there corresponding key continuities in organizational life? I concluded that the demarcation and defense of organizational boundaries could be used this way. As long as a boundary around a group of people included in the study was uninterruptedly maintained, I treated them as an ongoing organization, even if the composition, activities, outputs, and inputs of the group did not remain constant. When the borders became indistinguishable, I assumed all other evidences of collective life had diminished to the vanishing point also, and thereupon declared the organization deceased.

Of course, "boundary" is not a simple, clear concept. Organizational borders are permeable and movable; they may contract or expand, resist or permit traffic in or out. This variability makes their existence or disappearance difficult to establish. Still, there are some reasonably concrete indicators of boundaries—for example, visible symbols distinguishing an in-group from all others, rites of boundary crossing (induction and departure rites), perimeters of internal communications networks, evidences of organizational jurisdiction (e.g., the distribution of the burdens and benefits of membership).[2] I was not able to examine in detail every one of the 421 organizations comprehended by my research, so I cannot testify to the state of these indicators for every decision I had to make; my judgments were largely impressionistic. But this was the rule of thumb I employed, and it seemed to work satisfactorily.

2. Herbert Kaufman, "Why Organizations Behave as They Do," Papers Presented at an Interdisciplinary Seminar on Administrative Theory, University of Texas, March 20–21, 1961, pp. 40–42.

This means the "functions" of a government agency do not serve here as the hallmark of its existence. If you try to employ them for this purpose, you soon discover you can trace almost every bureau back to the eighteenth century; some clerk somewhere was doing something from time to time that foreshadowed the work of virtually every present organization. Conversely, many changes of function do not necessarily betoken death. The turn from poliomyelitis to birth defects by the National Foundation for Infantile Paralysis (now the National Foundation–March of Dimes), for instance, was a mark of its vitality, not of its demise. Similarly, abandonment of an original plan to rationalize railroad freight service in New York harbor in favor of facilitating motor traffic and mass transit did not signal the end of the Port of New York Authority (now the Port Authority of New York and New Jersey). Change of function and disruption of organizational boundaries often go hand in hand, but when they did not, the latter rather than the former was the controlling criterion of continuity in this research.

Only a small minority of the 421 cases examined presented difficult choices; the great majority were relatively unambiguous. Moreover, where dates were uncertain, the differences between the alternatives were frequently too small to have much effect on the research findings.

Nevertheless, there are numerous soft spots in the data. Since this is a small-scale venture into unknown territory, it ought to be used cautiously.

PROCEDURE

The choice of 1973 and 1923 as the dates for comparison was neither accidental nor arbitrary. In 1923 a predecessor of the Brookings Institution published a detailed history of the federal administrative structure,[3] which spelled out the growth of national administration department by department, bureau by bureau, including exhaustive references to the official instruments of creation and reorganization. In 1924 Congress received a report from the Joint Committee on the

3. Lloyd M. Short, *The Development of National Administrative Organization in the United States* (Johns Hopkins Press, 1923). The book was prepared under the auspices of the Institute for Government Research, one of three separate organizations joined in 1927 to form the Brookings Institution.

Reorganization of the Administrative Branch of the Government,[4] containing fairly complete charts. The following year George Cyrus Thorpe produced a tome that must be regarded as an antecedent of the official government manual that first appeared a decade later; conceived as a guide for lawyers whose practice required that they know their way around the federal government, it described with remarkable completeness the organization and history of every component of the government's administrative machinery.[5] As I was to discover, there were still units I could not adequately account for, obliging me to search through statutes, annual reports, the *Official Register of the United States*,[6] the *Congressional Directory*,[7] and histories of individual departments and bureaus.[8] But the task would have been overwhelming without the material collected and systematically organized by the diligent compilers of the overall record up to the early twenties, which is why I took 1923 as my first year.

Having resources for only one additional reading, I elected 1973 because I wanted a substantial interval between the two readings. Too short an interval could produce misleading results if the stretch of time were markedly atypical. And even if the period were not atypical, it might conceal long-term trends; a long view is needed to

4. *Reorganization of the Executive Departments*, S. Doc. 302, 67:4 (GPO, 1923).

5. *Federal Departmental Organization and Practice* (West, 1925).

6. The *Official Register* was a list of the occupants of federal administrative and supervisory positions organized by agencies and their subdivisions. It was published by various departments and bureaus from the early days of the Republic until 1959, when the *United States Government Manual* (see note 9) took over many of its functions.

7. The *Congressional Directory* has appeared under various titles since 1809; since 1865, it has been published by the Government Printing Office.

8. By and large, the official sources sufficed in most cases. To fill in gaps, however, I was helped especially by Graham H. Stuart, *The Department of State* (Macmillan, 1949); Gladys L. Baker and others, *Century of Service: The First 100 Years of the United States Department of Agriculture* (U.S. Department of Agriculture, 1963); Wayne D. Rasmussen and Gladys L. Baker, *The Department of Agriculture* (Praeger, 1972); Ralph C. Williams, *The United States Public Health Service, 1789–1950* (Commissioned Officers Association of the United States Public Health Service, 1951); U.S. Department of Labor, *The Anvil and the Plow: U.S. Department of Labor, 1913–63* (GPO, 1963); U.S. Department of the Treasury, *Department of the Treasury* (GPO, 1972); Luther A. Huston, *The Department of Justice* (Praeger, 1967); William Barnes, *The Foreign Service of the United States* (U.S. Department of State, 1961); Albert Langelutting, *The Department of Justice of the United States* (Johns Hopkins Press, 1927).

distinguish true invariance from gradual though significant development. Anyway, I was curious about recent developments. So a round half-century of experience had much to recommend it.

It also had one major drawback: relying on readings at each end of it would not capture the births and deaths of organizations created after 1923 that did not survive until 1973. Without these figures, the true death rate of young agencies cannot be determined conclusively. Although a clue to one of the possible factors in the dynamics of the federal organizational population would thus be lost, the loss would not preclude an answer to the question of immortality that is the central quest of this study. The fifty-year option was therefore chosen despite the drawback.

In the course of those fifty years, no comprehensive, historical survey of the whole federal administrative structure was published; Short and Thorpe started no trend. But in 1936 the *United States Government Manual*[9] got its start. The annual volumes in that series, the continuing flow of scholarly and popular histories,[10] and officers and employees of the departments and agencies, who went out of their way to be helpful, filled most of the gap.[11] Having to pull together the data from so many sources made compilation of the 1973 list much more difficult and time-consuming than the gathering of the 1923 list, but the materials were there and eventually the task was done.

One problem I did not anticipate was the introduction of possible

9. Now published annually in Washington by the Government Printing Office.

10. The Brookings Institution and its predecessor, the Institute for Government Research, published between 1917 and 1931 two series—Studies in Administration and Service Monographs—useful in reconstructing much administrative history at the federal level. More recently, Praeger Publishers undertook the Praeger Library of U.S. Government Departments and Agencies, a series to include over seventy titles, of which more than two dozen have already appeared. More generally, see the four-volume history by Leonard D. White, all published by Macmillan: *The Federalists* (1948), *The Jeffersonians* (1951), *The Jacksonians* (1954), and *The Republican Era* (1958). These treat the growth of federal administration to the beginning of the twentieth century.

11. In some departments, such as Agriculture, well-developed and expert historical offices were the repositories of needed information. But in others, offices of administrative management or of records services were the main source, and departmental libraries and librarians were invariably of great assistance. Finding the collections of relevant official documents therefore took some time and energy, there being no obvious, standardized location in every organization.

inconsistencies arising from changes in the status of some agencies in the course of the half-century. In 1923 each department and each of its major subdivisions were easily identified and counted; the criteria for inclusion in the sample were unambiguous. By 1973, however, some were lower in the hierarchy than they had been originally (either because they were demoted or, more commonly, because new administrative levels had been interposed between them and the top command). Several became independent or otherwise ceased to satisfy the criteria for inclusion applied to the 1923 reading. A few that were not high enough in 1923 to appear on the list were subsequently elevated, so that by 1973 they qualified for inclusion. In several instances, two bureaus were placed under a common command, raising questions about their subsequent status.

How should these changes in status be counted? The simplest solution would have been to drop them out of the study altogether, but this procedure could have skewed the results; casting inconvenient cases out of a sample is hardly sound practice. Another solution for organizations eligible for inclusion in one year but not in the other might have been to count them only in the year for which they qualified, but that would have changed the population base between readings and upset birth and death rate computations. I therefore included in both readings every organization alive in both years and eligible for inclusion in either the 1923 or the 1973 reading. That way, no organization in existence at the beginning and the end of the period was omitted from the sample merely because its position in the governmental structure had changed.

The classification difficulties engendered by the consolidation of bureaus, however, could not be so easily resolved by a simple decision rule. A consolidation can represent the death of one organization and the survival of the other, the death of both and the birth of a replacement for them, or the survival of both and the appearance of a new, more inclusive one as well. Each such event had to be decided individually. Fortunately, there were not many cases of this kind. In accordance with my policy of leaning over backwards to find continuity rather than turnover, my presumption ran in favor of the third interpretation (two survivors and a birth) unless there was strong evidence to the contrary. Occasionally, the evidence did indeed indicate amalgamation so extensive and dramatic that the second interpretation (two deaths) seemed unavoidable; the formation of the Foreign

Service out of the Diplomatic Bureau and the Consular Bureau of the State Department, for example, sounded the death knell of the fused components as discrete entities. More commonly, though, continuity prevailed.

At last, then, the data were arrayed and ready for analysis. The next chapter summarizes the raw findings and the evidence behind them. The final chapter explores the implications of the findings.

FINDINGS AND EVIDENCE

THE GOVERNMENT ORGANIZATIONS EXAMINED DO INDEED DISPLAY IM-
PRESSIVE POWERS OF ENDURANCE (table 1).

There were 175 organizations in the 1923 sample. No less than 148
of them (nearly 85 percent) were still going in 1973 (including 31
now at lower administrative levels and 8 no longer in executive departments). Only 27 (a little over 15 percent) disappeared. Thus the
chances that an organization alive in 1923 would still be alive in 1973
were very high. Indeed, the chances that an organization in the 1923
sample would be not only alive in 1973 but in virtually the same
status were quite good; 109 of the original 175 (over 62 percent, or
better than three out of five) were in this situation.

BIRTHS OF NEW ORGANIZATIONS INCREASED SUFFICIENTLY AFTER 1923
TO BALANCE OFF THE AGING OF THE LARGE NUMBER OF OLDER, ENDUR-
ING UNITS.

In a population of any kind, if no new members were added, the
average age of those that survived obviously would go up annually.
Only an offsetting infusion of new blood could keep the average age
from rising.

The average age of the organizations examined in this study remained remarkably stable (table 1). Although many of the organizations alive in 1923 were established when the first government took
office under the Constitution in 1789, 134 years earlier, the median
age of the group was only 27. Most of the 1923 group survived to
1973, which meant that a substantial number of organizations at
least 50 and as much as 184 years old were scattered among the 394
organizations in the 1973 population. Nevertheless, the median age
remained 27. Youth just balanced age.

This stability is only partly accounted for by the addition of three
executive departments—Health, Education, and Welfare; Housing
and Urban Development; and Transportation—and the Executive
Office of the President to the rosters between the boundary years. To
be sure, they and their post-1923 subdivisions comprised 80 units

34

TABLE 1. *Organizational Births, Deaths, and Survivors, by Age Group, 1923–73*[a]

| Age group | 1923 population[b] | Deaths, 1924–73 | | | Number surviving in 1973[b] | Number surviving from 1923[c] | Births, 1924–73[c] | 1973 population[c] |
		By age in 1923	As percent of 1923 population	By age at death				
0–9	35	8	23	3	27	...	120	120
10–19	38	5	13	5	33	...	33	33
20–29	17	2	12	1	15	...	56	56
30–39	15	2	13	2	13	...	30	30
40–49	10	2	20	3	8	...	7	7
50–59	16	2	13	3	14	27	...	27
60–69	13	2	15	2	11	33	...	33
70–79	8	0	0	2	8	15	...	15
80–89	2	1	50	0	1	13	...	13
90–99	6	2	33	4	4	8	...	8
100–109	2	0	0	1	2	14	...	14
110–119	2	0	0	0	2	11	...	11
120–129	0	0	...	0	0	8	...	8
130–139	11	1	9	0	10	1	...	1
140–149	...	...	...	0	...	4	...	4
150–159	...	...	...	1	...	2	...	2
160–169	...	...	...	0	...	2	...	2
170–179	...	...	...	0	...	0	...	0
180–184	...	...	...	0	...	10	...	10
Total	175	27	...	27	148	148	246	394
Median age	27	22	...	44	27	77	10	27

a. The terms "births," "deaths," and "population" are explained in the text.
b. Organizations assigned to age groups by their age in 1923.
c. Organizations assigned to age groups by their age in 1973.

with a median age of 6 (table 2), which certainly helped hold down the average age of the 1973 population. But to keep that average at the same level as in 1923 required much more. New organizations had to have appeared in profusion throughout the system to produce this result.

And so they did (see table 2). Within the original seven departments, 166 new units were created from 1924 to 1973, and they had a

TABLE 2. Changes in Organization Population and Median Age, by Department, 1923–73

| | Organizations | | | | | | | Median age | | | | |
| | 1923 population | 1924–73 | | | | | 1973 population | 1923 population | 1924–73 | | | 1973 population[b] |
Department		Deaths	Transfers out	Transfers in	Survivors	Births			Deaths[a]	Survivors[a]	Births[b]	
State	26	4	0	1	23	18	41	17.5	52[e]	20	28	54
Treasury	28	2	5	0	21	31	52	55.5	53	60	12	29
Justice	24	1	4	2	21	11	32	19.5	1[d]	20	9	59
Interior	29	4	9	3	19	36	55	54	34.5[e]	44	9	23
Agriculture	32	11	3	0	18	31	49	28	13	30.5	20	34
Commerce	16	4	1	4	15	16	31	20	62[e]	20	4.5	34
Labor	17	1	4	1	13	22	35	10	5[d]	10	9	26
Independent[c]	1	0	1	8	8	0[e]	8	…	…	…	…	…
Other	2	0	1	0	1	1	2	…	…	…	…	…
Subtotal	175	27	28	19	139	166	305	…	…	…	…	…
Median age	27[a]	22[a]	…	…	23[a]	11.5[b]	36[b]	…	…	…	…	…

Housing and Urban Development	⋯	⋯	0	0	19	19	⋯	⋯	⋯	20	20
Transportation	⋯	⋯	2	2	21	23	⋯	⋯	81.5[c]	6	6
Health, Education, and Welfare	⋯	⋯	5	5	26	31	⋯	⋯	53[c]	17	20
Executive Office of the President	⋯	⋯	2	2	14	16	⋯	⋯	34[c]	3.5	6.5
Subtotal	⋯	⋯	9	9	80	89	⋯	⋯	⋯	⋯	⋯
Median age	22[a]	⋯	⋯	⋯	6[b]	8[a]	⋯	⋯	⋯	⋯	⋯
Total	175	28	28	148	246	304	⋯	⋯	⋯	20	20
Median age	27[a]	⋯	⋯	27[a]	10[b]	27[b]	⋯	⋯	⋯	6	6

a. Age in 1923.

b. Age in 1973.

c. Few cases, wide dispersion; median not significant.

d. One case.

e. One independent in 1923 moved into a department. Eight in departments became or were transferred to independent agencies. No other independent agencies are in the sample.

median age of only 11.5 years. Consequently, the median age of all the units making up the original seven departments went from 27 in 1923 to only 36 in 1973, a modest rise for a half-century of elapsed time. Clearly, then, it was not just the establishment of vast new structures outside the original seven that held the general average age down; the same thing was taking place inside the old ones too.

The rate at which organizations were created was dramatically higher after 1923 than before. Of the units composing the 1923 population, 115 had been established during the preceding fifty years, or at an average rate of 2.3 units a year. Of the units alive in 1973, 246 had been set up during the preceding fifty years, or at an average rate of almost 5 a year. That is why the median age remained so stable; for some reason—or perhaps purely by chance—the rate rose just enough to keep it almost constant.

STAFF ORGANIZATIONS INCREASED A LITTLE MORE RAPIDLY THAN LINE UNITS (table 3).

One of the most common distinctions drawn among organizations is the difference between line and staff units. Line units are usually defined as those that produce the characteristic end-products or services of the organization to which they belong. Staff units provide products or services that facilitate the work of the line components but do not in themselves constitute the major output of the parent organization.

The distinction is not free of ambiguity. In relation to the government as a whole, an agency may be clearly staff (the Civil Service Commission, for example) or line (the Department of Labor, for instance) yet comprise components that are both line and staff in relation to itself. The level of analysis has much to do with how an organization is classified. In the main, however, the assignment of organizations in this study to these categories seemed a straightforward task. Only a relatively small number of units displayed both line and staff traits equally; such units were identified as "mixed." While some of the classifications might be disputed by other observers, the vast majority are probably not controversial.

In 1923, 64 percent of the 175 organizations in the sample were in the line. By 1973 the proportion of line units in the 394 organizations in the sample had declined to under 58 percent. At the same time, 8 percent of the 1923 sample were of a mixed character. By 1973 this percentage had dropped to 4. Meanwhile, staff units rose from 28 percent in 1923 to 38 percent in 1973. The ratio of unmixed line to unmixed staff units, 2.25 to 1 in 1923, thus fell to 1.5 to 1 in 1973. The movement is not an avalanche, but it is certainly distinct.

These changes came about largely because staff units constituted a heavy proportion of all the organizations created after 1923. Between 1923 and 1973, 246 organizations were established; 42 percent were staff and 2 percent were mixed; only 56 percent were line. In addition, of the 27 organizations that died after 1923, 81 percent had been in the line. Staff units were achieving a rising birth rate while line units were falling off sharply.

The disproportionately high representation of line organizations among the fatalities (81 percent of the deaths though they constituted only 64 percent of the 1923 population) is not easily explained; it may be a general phenomenon or a unique feature of the samples here examined. The rising proportion of staff organizations, however, is not surprising. The multiplication of units throughout the system apparently gives many administrators the feeling that their influence on their subordinates has been diluted. To reassert control, they increase the number of staff units in their own offices, the logic being that such units share their perspectives to a greater extent than subordinate line organizations do and so will correct deviations from leadership policies—or will at least maintain surveillance and alert leaders to such deviations. Even if this strategy does not fulfill all the expectations for it, the jurisdictions of the staff agencies cut across the jurisdictions of the line agencies in so many different ways that the agencies end up curbing each other as they negotiate settlements and understandings; the effect is to keep everybody within bounds despite the attenuation of leadership attention induced by high organizational birth rates, thereby allowing leaders to concentrate on problem areas without having everything else get out of hand.[1] Increasing staff units does not invariably produce the intended effects, but the practice enjoys so much confidence that it has contributed heavily to the rapid growth of the staff sector in recent decades.

1. Herbert Kaufman, *The Limits of Organizational Change* (University of Alabama Press, 1971), pp. 35–36; Herbert A. Simon, Donald W. Smithburg, and Victor A. Thompson, *Public Administration* (Knopf, 1950), pp. 272–79, 291–94.

TABLE 3. Organizations, by Department and Type, 1923–73

Department	1923 population			Deaths, 1924–73			Survivors, 1923–73[a]			Births, 1924–73			1973 population		
	Line	Staff	Mixed	Line	Staff	Mixed	Line	Staff	Mixed	Line	Staff	Mixed	Line	Staff	Mixed
State															
Number	17	9	0	3	1	0	14	9	0	9	9	0	23	18	0
Percent	65	35	0	75	25	0	61	39	0	50	50	0	56	44	0
Treasury															
Number	21	7	0	1	1	0	16	5	0	13	18	0	29	23	0
Percent	75	25	0	50	50	0	76	24	0	42	58	0	56	44	0
Justice															
Number	4	8	12	1	0	0	6	4	11	9	1	1	15	5	12
Percent	17	33	50	100	0	0	29	19	52	82	9	9	47	16	37
Interior															
Number	22	7	0	2	2	0	13	6	0	17	19	0	30	25	0
Percent	76	24	0	50	50	0	68	32	0	47	53	0	55	45	0
Agriculture															
Number	24	7	1	10	0	1	11	7	0	21	9	1	32	16	1
Percent	75	22	3	91	0	9	61	39	0	68	29	3	65	33	2
Commerce															
Number	10	5	1	4	0	0	8	6	1	12	3	1	20	9	2
Percent	63	31	6	100	0	0	53	40	7	75	19	6	65	29	6

	1	2	3	4	5	6	7	8	9	10	11	12	13	14	15
Labor															
Number	12	5	0	1	0	0	7	6	0	11	10	1	18	16	1
Percent	11	29	0	100	0	0	54	46	0	50	45	5	51	46	3
Housing and Urban Development															
Number	…	…	…	…	…	0	0	0	0	10	9	0	10	9	0
Percent	…	…	…	…	…	0	0	0	0	53	47	0	53	47	0
Transportation															
Number	…	…	…	…	…	2	0	0	2	12	8	1	14	8	1
Percent	…	…	…	…	…	100	0	0	100	57	38	5	61	35	4
Health, Education, and Welfare															
Number	…	…	…	…	…	0	5	0	0	17	9	0	22	9	0
Percent	…	…	…	…	…	0	100	0	0	65	35	0	71	29	0
Executive Office of the President															
Number	…	…	…	…	…	0	0	2	0	5	9	0	5	11	0
Percent	…	…	…	…	…	0	0	100	0	36	64	0	31	69	0
Independent															
Number	1	0	0	0	0	0	8	0	0	0	0	0	8	0	0
Other															
Number	1	1	0	0	0	0	1	0	0	1	0	0	2	0	0
Total number	112[b]	49	14[b]	22[b]	4	1[b]	91[b]	45	12[b]	137	104	5	228	149	17
Percent of total	64	28	8	81	15	4	62	30	8	56	42	2	58	38	4

a. Net after transfers. See table 2.
b. Discrepancies in row totals are due to the shift of one organization from mixed to line status between 1923 and 1973.

STATUTES WERE GIVING WAY TO EXECUTIVE AND ADMINISTRATIVE
FORMS OF ACTION AS THE LEGAL INSTRUMENTS BY WHICH AGENCIES
ARE CREATED (table 4).

Of the 175 organizations in the 1923 sample, statutes underlay
two-thirds. Of the 394 organizations in the 1973 sample, statutes
were behind only 39 percent.

Departmental orders, which accounted for only one-third of the
1923 sample, were the origin of over half the 1973 sample. In addition, reorganization plans, nonexistent in 1923, gave rise to almost 7
percent of the 1973 group, executive orders of the President set up
another 3 percent, while the final 1 percent owed life to other legal
instruments.[2]

Obviously, nonstatutory forms gained strikingly in popularity
after 1923. Only 21 percent of the 246 organizations born after 1923
were established by statute. Departmental orders, by contrast, created 62 percent, reorganization plans another 11 percent, executive
orders 4 percent, and other forms the remaining 1 percent. For adding to the administrative structure of the government, statutes were
no longer the favored method.

STATUTES DID NOT CONTRIBUTE MUCH MORE TO ORGANIZATIONAL
DURABILITY THAN DID OTHER INSTRUMENTS OF ESTABLISHMENT (tables
4 and 5).

In 1923 the median age of the organizations set up by statute was
forty years. In 1973 it was sixty-five years. Yet the median ages of the
total population in 1923 and 1973 were the same. A seeming implication is that statutory organizations enjoy higher protection than organizations given life by other forms. The implication is reinforced
by the differentials: organizations created by statute constituted 66
percent of the total 1923 population but only 56 percent of the organizations that died in the next fifty years; conversely, organizations
created by departmental action made up only 33 percent of the 1923
population but 44 percent of the group that died. Eighty-seven percent of the statutory organizations survived from 1923 to 1973 as

2. The Constitution (in the case of the President), presidential memoranda
in the case of two components of the Executive Office. The *United States Government Manual* cites no official source for the creation of the Office of the Vice President; apparently, it was set up by the assignment of space and personnel by the
President.

against only 79 percent of the departmentally created units. The chances for statutory organizations thus seem better than those for their less fortunate fellows.

But the evidence is not as unequivocal as it might appear. The main reason the average age of statutory units increased was that so few (21 percent) of the organizations established after 1923 were set up by specific legislation; had the additions been made by statute, they would have reduced the average age of statutory organizations. In other words, it was not necessarily the greater *durability* of the statutory agencies but the new preference for administrative and executive instruments that produced the rise in their age.

Furthermore, for the survivors from 1923 to 1973, almost the same proportions of departmental and statutory units as in the total 1923 population obtained. Sixty-eight percent of the survivors were statutory, as against 66 percent for the 1923 group, and 31 percent departmental, as against 33 percent. The shift was trivial; the ratios hardly changed. Statutory units did not fare significantly better.

Indeed, statutory organizations proved vulnerable to elimination by nonstatutory action. Of the twenty-seven deaths of organizations covered in the study, eighteen occurred through departmental action, three by executive order, and one by reorganization plan; only five were accomplished by statute. Thirteen of the fifteen statutory units that died between 1923 and 1973 were terminated by nonstatutory legal instruments (thanks largely to the delegation of authority to department heads described in the first chapter).

In short, whatever added protection statutes may once have afforded the agencies they set up, the advantage was apparently declining. Statutory bodies were no more likely to escape elimination than agencies dependent on other legal instruments.

MANY OF THE TRENDS OBSERVED IN ALL THE ORGANIZATIONS TAKEN TOGETHER MANIFESTED THEMSELVES ALSO IN INDIVIDUAL DEPARTMENTS, BUT NOT ALL TRENDS APPEARED IN ALL DEPARTMENTS.

This finding applies only to the seven departments in both the 1923 and 1973 readings, the ones established after 1923 (the Executive Office of the President and the Departments of Health, Education, and Welfare, Housing and Urban Development, and Transportation) providing no basis for such a comparison.

Some of the broad tendencies of the total organizational popula-

TABLE 4. *Organizations by Instrument of Creation and Department, 1923–73*[a]

Department	1923 population Stat.	D.O.	Other	Total	Deaths, 1924–73[b] Stat.	D.O.	Total	Deaths as percent of total	Survivors, 1923–73[c] Stat.	D.O.	Other	Total
State												
Number	10	16	0	26	0	4	4	...	11	12	0	23
Percent	38	62	0	100	0	100	100	15	48	52	0	100
Treasury												
Number	23	5	0	28	2	0	2	...	17	4	0	21
Percent	82	18	0	100	100	0	100	7	81	19	0	100
Justice												
Number	16	8	0	24	0	1	1	...	14	7	0	21
Percent	67	33	0	100	0	100	100	4	67	33	0	100
Interior												
Number	23	6	0	29	3	1	4	...	13	6	0	19
Percent	79	21	0	100	75	25	100	14	68	32	0	100
Agriculture												
Number	18	14	0	32	6	5	11	...	11	7	0	18
Percent	56	44	0	100	55	45	100	34	61	39	0	100
Commerce												
Number	13	3	0	16	4	0	4	...	12	3	0	15
Percent	81	19	0	100	100	0	100	25	80	20	0	100
Labor												
Number	11	6	0	17	0	1	1	...	9	4	0	13
Percent	65	35	0	100	0	100	100	6	69	31	0	100
Housing and Urban Development												
Number	...	...	...	...	...	...	...	...	0	0	0	0
Percent	...	...	...	...	...	...	...	...	0	0	0	0
Transportation												
Number	...	...	...	...	...	...	...	...	1	1	0	2
Percent	...	...	...	...	...	...	...	...	50	50	0	100
Health, Education, and Welfare												
Number	...	...	...	...	...	...	...	...	4	1	0	5
Percent	...	...	...	...	...	...	...	...	80	20	0	100
Executive Office of the President												
Number	...	...	...	...	...	...	...	...	2	0	0	2
Percent	...	...	...	...	...	...	...	...	100	0	0	100
Independent[d]												
Number	1	0	0	1	0	0	0	0	7	1	0	8
Percent	100	0	0	100	0	0	0	0	88	12	0	100
Other												
Number	1	0	1	2	0	0	0	0	0	0	1	1
Total number	116	58	1	175	15	12	27	...	101	46	1	148
Percent of total	66	33	1	100	56	44	100	15	68	31	1	100
Median age	40[e]	14[e]	134[e]	27[e]	39[e]	14.5[e]	22[e]	...	41[e]	14[e]	134[e]	27[e]

a. Stat. = statute; D.O. = departmental order; R.P. = reorganization plan; E.O. = executive order.

b. By instruments of creation, not of termination.

c. Net after transfers. See table 2.

d. One independent in 1923 moved into a department. Eight in departments became,

	Births, 1924-73						1973 population				
Stat.	D.O.	R.P.	E.O.	Other	Total	Stat.	D.O.	R.P.	E.O.	Other	Total
3	13	0	2	0	18	14	25	0	2	0	41
17	72	0	11	0	100	34	61	0	5	0	100
4	26	1	0	0	31	21	30	1	0	0	52
13	84	3	0	0	100	40	58	2	0	0	100
3	6	1	1	0	11	17	13	1	1	0	32
27	55	9	9	0	100	53	41	3	3	0	100
7	26	3	0	0	36	20	32	3	0	0	55
20	72	8	0	0	100	36	58	6	0	0	100
6	20	3	2	0	31	17	27	3	2	0	49
19	65	10	6	0	100	35	55	6	4	0	100
3	11	2	0	0	16	15	14	2	0	0	31
19	69	12	0	0	100	48	45	7	0	0	100
3	17	2	0	0	22	12	21	2	0	0	35
14	77	9	0	0	100	34	60	6	0	0	100
1	16	2	0	0	19	1	16	2	0	0	19
5	84	11	0	0	100	5	84	11	0	0	100
11	7	3	0	0	21	12	8	3	0	0	23
52	34	4	0	0	100	52	35	13	0	0	100
6	11	8	1	0	26	10	12	8	1	0	31
23	42	31	4	0	100	32	39	26	3	0	100
5	0	2	5	2	14	7	0	2	5	2	16
36	0	14	36	14	100	44	0	13	31	13	100
0	0	0	0	0	0	7	1	0	0	0	8
0	0	0	0	0	0	88	12	0	0	0	100
0	0	0	0	1	1	0	0	0	0	2	2
52	153	27	11	3	246	153	199	27	11	4	394
21	62	11	5	1	100	39	51	7	3	1	100
18f	8f	20f	23f	0	10f	65f	12f	20f	23f	g	27f

or were transferred to, independent agencies. No other independent agencies are in the sample.

e. Age in 1923.

f. Age in 1973.

g. Ages are 0, 0, 2, and 184.

TABLE 5. *Deaths of Organizations, by Instruments of Termination and of Creation, 1924–73*

Instrument of creation	Instrument of termination				
	Statute	Departmental action	Executive order	Reorganization plan	Total
Statute	2	9	3	1	15
Departmental action	3	9	0	0	12
Total	5	18	3	1	27

tion covered by this study emerged within the seven departments individually, but the departments also displayed substantial variation in some respects.

First, the death rate in each of the seven departments was low (table 4). In three departments it was below 10 percent; in two, 14 and 15 percent. In Commerce it reached 25 percent. The Department of Agriculture had an exceptionally high rate—34 percent, more than double the rate for the population of all the departments collectively—but one that still meant the chances of its components' surviving were twice as good as their chances of going under.

Second, in all seven departments, the proportion of constituent units established by statute declined between 1923 and 1973 (table 4). The decline was smallest, 4 percentage points, in the State Department (in part because the State Department was the only one in 1923 that had more departmentally created units than statutory units). In the Departments of Justice and Agriculture, the decline was moderate (14 and 21 percentage points, respectively) but still distinct. In the remaining four departments, it was pronounced, exceeding 30 percentage points in every case.

Third, in five of the seven departments, the proportion of staff units in the total went up between the two readings (table 3). In the Department of Commerce, it declined very slightly, from 31 to 29 percent. Only in the Department of Justice did it fall sharply. (That department, being in large part a staff organization, had an exceptionally high ratio of staff and mixed components in 1923. Moreover, an extraordinarily high proportion of the additions to it after 1923 were line units. The two factors combined produced its statistically atypical pattern.)

But even the weak tendency toward higher survival rates for older organizations discernible in the total 1923 population cannot be detected in the individual departments because there are so few cases and so much dispersion in each cell in table 2. Hence not much reliance can be placed on the finding that the median age of survivors from 1923 to 1973 was higher than the median age of the units that died in five of the cases—especially since the opposite tendency in the other two cases, though they rest on equally unreliable data, is strong.

Nor did the median ages of the components of the seven departments remain stable over the five decades (table 2) as the median of the total population did. In two departments (State and Justice) the figures were thirty and thirty-six years higher in 1973; in three (Agriculture, Commerce, and Labor) they were up six to sixteen years; in two (Treasury and Interior) they were down more than twenty-six years.

As is so often true, therefore, the figures for the whole population conceal variations among the subsets, so that inferences must be drawn with great caution.

THE GROWTH OF THE EXECUTIVE BRANCH, AS EXEMPLIFIED BY THE ORGANIZATIONS COVERED IN THIS STUDY, WAS NOT A STEADY PROCESS BUT PROCEEDED IN SPURTS (table 6; figures 1 and 2).

From the very start of the Republic, expansions of the organizational population of the executive branch (and of individual departments as well) came in bursts of creativity interspersed among periods of relative quiescence. The absolute number of new organizations set up in the periods of peak activity tended to rise over time; as the twentieth century wore on, the levels of the peaks reached higher and higher (figure 1), reflecting the growing diversity and intensity of the tasks of the federal government.

The variability of the growth process is evident from the percentage figures as well as from the absolute numbers (figure 2). The oscillations in the percentages were pronounced from the beginning, when the absolute number of organizations extant in any presidential term was smaller than in later terms and when a relatively modest increase in any number therefore constituted a large proportional rise. Despite the expansion of the base, however, the percentage changes continued to vary in much the same way in later periods,

TABLE 6. *Births and Deaths of Organizations, by Presidential Term, 1789–1973*[a]

Presidential term	Births	Deaths[b]	Net increase or decrease	Cumulative total	Percentage increase or decrease
1789–92	11	...	...	...	...
1793–96	0	...	0	11	0
1797–1800	0	...	0	11	0
1801–04	0	...	0	11	0
1805–08	1	...	1	12	9
1809–12	1	...	1	13	8
1813–16	0	...	0	13	0
1817–20	2	...	2	15	15
1821–24	1	...	1	16	7
1825–28	0	...	0	16	0
1829–32	1	...	1	17	6
1833–36	5	...	5	22	29
1837–40	1	...	1	23	5
1841–44	0	...	0	23	0
1845–48	0	...	0	23	0
1849–52	4	...	4	27	17
1853–56	5	...	5	32	19
1857–60	2	...	2	34	6
1861–64	11	...	11	45	32
1865–68	5	...	5	50	11
1869–72	10	...	10	60	20
1873–76	4	...	4	64	7
1877–80	4	...	4	68	6
1881–84	5	...	5	73	7
1885–88	4	...	4	77	5
1889–92	7	...	7	84	9
1893–96	4	...	4	88	5
1897–1900	2	...	2	90	2
1901–04	15	...	15	105	17
1905–08	9	...	9	114	9
1909–12	15	...	15	129	13
1913–16	17	...	17	146	13
1917–20	16	...	16	162	11
1921–24	14	4	10	172	6
1925–28	3	5	−2	170	−1

TABLE 6 (continued)

Presidential term	Births	Deaths[b]	Net increase or decrease	Cumu- lative total	Per- centage increase or decrease
1929–32	0	0	0	170	0
1933–36	11	3	8	178	5
1937–40	20	2	18	196	10
1941–44	9	4	5	201	3
1945–48	22	0	22	223	11
1949–52	13	3	10	233	4
1953–56	22	6	16	249	7
1957–60	4	0	4	253	2
1961–64	28	0	28	281	11
1965–68	33	0	33	314	12
1969–72	57	0	57	371	18
1973	23	0	23	394	6

a. Data do not include organizations that were born and died between 1923 and 1973.
b. Mortality figures for 1924–73 only.

the size of the absolute changes more or less keeping pace with the size of the total population. Except for two terms when the increases exceeded 20 percent and one when there was a decrease, all the variation has been between zero and 20 percent, changes in the base notwithstanding.

In general, the greatest growth in the organizational population covered in this study seems to coincide with the terms of presidents commonly regarded as strong and innovative by other standards, and the quiescent periods—especially in the middle and late twenties —also coincide with other indicators of inactivity. There are, how- ever, many exceptions to this pattern. The surges in the Taylor- Fillmore, Pierce, and Grant administrations would not ordinarily be anticipated. The New Deal does not loom as large as one might have expected, but that is principally because many of its creations were not in the executive departments and were therefore outside the scope of this inquiry. The extraordinary activity of the Nixon admin- istration is something of a surprise because of its announced hostility to the federal bureaucracy; the creation of new agencies is not neces-

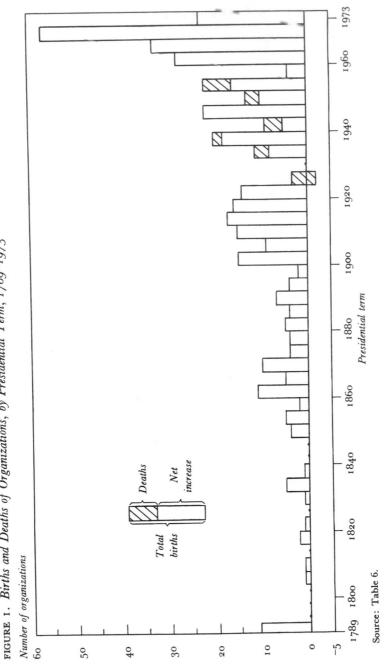

FIGURE 1. *Births and Deaths of Organizations, by Presidential Term, 1789–1973*

Source: Table 6.

FIGURE 2. *Percentage Change in Organizational Population in Each Presidential Term, 1789–1973* [a]

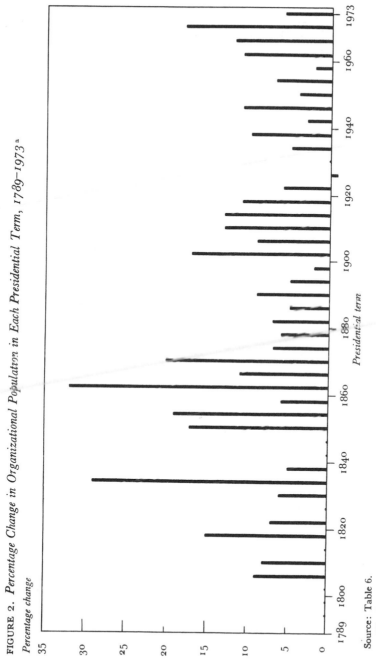

Source: Table 6.

a. The bars are at the midpoint of each presidential term.

sarily inconsistent with such an outlook, but it is not the conventional image of an antibureaucratic strategy.[3]

Nor does the party affiliation of a president seem to predict the rate of organizational growth during his term of office. Republicans and Democrats both have had their share of activists, though a few more Republicans than Democrats were in power during the comparatively inactive stretches of the past hundred years.

These figures and findings, however, must be viewed with caution. Since the data come only from 1923 and 1973, many births are excluded; organizations that died before 1923 and those born after 1923 that died before 1973 do not appear. Moreover, the exclusion of agencies outside the executive departments omits many births; many New Deal and war agencies were in this category. At best, therefore, the indications are merely suggestive. But at least one thing may be fairly confidently inferred from this evidence and from what we know of the 1924–73 period: the growth of the federal organizational population does take place in fits and starts.

DEATHS, TOO, ARE UNEVENLY SPACED, AND THEY OCCUR AT A LOWER RATE THAN BUSINESS FAILURES, THOUGH NOT AT A TRIVIAL RATE (tables 6 and 7).

Deaths occurred in clusters. All of them were grouped in only fourteen of the fifty years from 1924 to 1973, though they were spread over a half-dozen presidential terms. A run of terminations was completed in the early years, but thereafter they were rather sporadic. It is difficult to perceive any pattern in timing.

The government organizations studied, however, did enjoy a lower death rate than businesses. In some respects, the comparison is forced, for there are millions of businesses and failures in the tens of thousands, whereas this study deals with only a few hundred government units and deaths in the tens. Converting the government organizational death rate into the standard measurement of business failure—failures per 10,000 businesses—much magnifies the impact of every individual government termination; on this basis a single death in any year constitutes a high rate. Despite these shortcomings, as a rough indication of the relation between the two populations, the comparison is helpful.

3. For an explanation of this strategy, see Richard P. Nathan, *The Plot That Failed: Nixon and the Administrative Presidency* (Wiley, 1975).

TABLE 7. *Deaths and Death Rates of Organizations Compared with Business Failure Rates, 1924–73*

Year	Organizations Deaths	Organizations Deaths per 10,000[a]	Business failures per 10,000 firms	Year	Organizations Deaths	Organizations Deaths per 10,000[a]	Business failures per 10,000 firms
1924	4	229	100	1950	1	44	34
1925	0	0	100	1951	0	0	31
1926	2	116	101	1952	2	86	29
1927	2	116	106	1953	5	215	33
1928	1	59	109	1954	0	0	42
1929	0	0	104	1955	1	41	42
1930	0	0	122	1956	0	0	48
1931	0	0	133	1957	0	0	52
1932	0	0	154	1958	0	0	56
1933	2	118	100	1959	0	0	52
1934	1	58	61	1960	0	0	57
1935	0	0	62	1961	0	0	64
1936	0	0	48	1962	0	0	61
1937	0	0	46	1963	0	0	56
1938	1	55	61	1964	0	0	53
1939	1	53	70	1965	0	0	53
1940	0	0	63	1966	0	0	52
1941	2	102	55	1967	0	0	49
1942	2	104	45	1968	0	0	39
1943	0	0	16	1969	0	0	37
1944	0	0	7	1970	0	0	44
1945	0	0	4	1971	0	0	42
1946	0	0	5	1972	0	0	38
1947	0	0	14	1973	0	0	36
1948	0	0	20				
1949	0	0	34	*Average*	0.54	27.6	56.8

Sources (business data): U.S. Bureau of the Census, *Historical Statistics of the United States: Colonial Times to 1957* (GPO, 1960); *Historical Statistics . . . Continuation to 1962* (GPO, 1965); *Statistical Abstract of the United States, 1965, 1968,* and *1974.*

a. Converted to the standard measurement of business failures—number per 10,000 units.

It shows that a common belief about them is justified. In any given year, because of the magnification of each case in the government population, the rate exceeded all but the very highest annual business failure rates. But when the figures were averaged over the half-century, the annual rate of business failures (56.8 per 10,000) was more than twice the annual death rate (27.9 per 10,000) of the government units.

At the same time, it should be noted that the government rate was not so low as to provide the complete certainty of survival that some observers imply they enjoy. Risks were smaller, but they did exist. They may, in fact, be greater than these figures suggest because it is possible that the evidence is skewed by taking readings fifty years apart. Since many organizations undoubtedly were born and died in that interval without leaving a record in the specimen population, the mortality figures may be abnormally low, much as vital statistics of a human population would be distorted by omitting infant and child mortality and by concentrating on the residents of old-age homes. Without more frequent readings, this possibility cannot be dismissed.

Certainly, there is ample reason to *suspect* that many mortalities occur among new organizations in the federal system. The New Deal, the Second World War, and the Korean War, for example, gave rise to many agencies that lived for brief periods; the initials of dissolved units—NRA, WPA, PWA, FERA, CCC, NYA, OPA, WPB, OWM, OWMR, WRA, ODM, ESA, OPS, WSB[4]—are like the bleached skeletons of bodies that once occupied the center of the governmental arena but soon expired. Their records buried in the National Archives, their obituaries simple entries in an appendix of the *Government Manual*,[5] they slip from memory, remembered only by the veterans who served in them.

4. National Recovery Administration; Works Progress Administration; Public Works Administration; Federal Emergency Relief Administration; Civilian Conservation Corps; National Youth Administration; Office of Price Adminstration; War Production Board; Office of War Mobilization; Office of War Mobilization and Reconversion; War Relocation Administration; Office of Defense Mobilization; Economic Stabilization Agency; Office of Price Stabilization; Wage Stabilization Board.

5. Appendix A, "Executive Agencies and Functions of the Federal Government Abolished, Transferred, or Terminated Subsequent to March 4, 1933," of the *Government Manual* includes a brief history of each agency covered. This may

Perhaps the death rate of the government organizational population is thus underestimated. But even if it is not, even if the figures are accurate as they stand, the rate is by no means negligible.

AMONG THE ORGANIZATIONS THAT DIED, SIX OF THE SEVEN HAZARDS TO ORGANIZATIONAL EXISTENCE APPEARED AS CAUSES OF DEATH. OVERALL, HOWEVER, CHANCE SEEMS TO HAVE PLAYED A LARGE PART IN THEIR TERMINATION.

It is not difficult to offer explanations for the deaths of the twenty-seven organizations that went out of existence between 1923 and 1973. Three, for example, may have been victims of leadership miscalculation: they were short-lived experiments that never took root. In the Department of Agriculture in the early twenties, there was apparently a plan to subject all the components of the department to multiple supervision of the kind advocated by Frederick W. Taylor.[6] Each unit was to be answerable for its scientific activities to a single departmental "director of scientific work," for its regulatory functions to a "director of regulatory work," and for its extension services to a "director of extension work." Apparently, the powerful bureaus were not very responsive to the new layer of supervision. The director of extension work ended as leader of the Extension Service and the descendants of that position can be found today. The other two, however, became nearly empty shells and were dropped formally in 1934 and 1939, respectively. Similarly, in the State Department, a Division of Political and Economic Information appeared in the ferment following World War I, but it sank without a trace a few years later.

Changes in political leadership and philosophy evidently contributed significantly to the deaths of others. Secretary of Agriculture Ezra Taft Benson was critical of the "swollen . . . bureaucracy" in his department, and on assuming office announced promptly that it was

come as close to the "coroner" mentioned in note 1, p. 27, as is possible in the federal setting.

6. Taylor, generally recognized as the father of scientific management, advocated replacement of "the old-fashioned single foreman by eight different men, each of whom has his own special duties." He called this "functional management," describing it as a method of taking advantage of the expertise that comes with specialization; see *The Principles of Scientific Management* (Harper, 1916), pp. 122 ff.; *Shop Management* (Harper, 1911), p. 99. "Taylorism," through the Taylor Society (eventually renamed the Society for the Advancement of Management), enjoyed a great vogue following the appearance of these works.

in for a major overhaul; his attitude and the restructuring it spawned doubtless explain why five bureaus in this survey (Agricultural and Industrial Chemistry, a descendant of the Bureau of Chemistry; Entomology and Plant Quarantine, a descendant of the Bureau of Entomology; Animal Industry; Plant Industry, Soils, and Agricultural Engineering, a descendant of the Bureau of Plant Industry; and Agricultural Economics) lost their organizational identities in 1953, the first year of his administration.

But the Department of Agriculture seemed to be testing patterns of organization for a long time. It underwent substantial change in 1938, when Secretary Henry A. Wallace searched for a structure that would coordinate its programs when they reached the farm. That was when the Bureau of Chemistry and Soils was broken up, and the soils component, the descendant of the Bureau of Soils, was divided among other units. In 1927 and 1928 Secretary William M. Jardine tried to separate research from regulation, which contributed to the demise of the Insecticide and Fungicide Board and the Federal Horticultural Board, as new organizations combining their functions and similar functions from other agencies absorbed them bit by bit until their structural identity vanished.

The Department of Agriculture thus had an unusually large number of organizational fatalities compared with the other six departments in the original sample. There is no self-evident reason why this should be so. Perhaps the rapid advances in agricultural sciences and technology led to swifter obsolescence of traditional structures than was the case in the other departments. Perhaps the technicians in the technical bureaus and their external allies saw in the changes in administrative organization no threat to their major interests, so the secretaries could feel free to experiment boldly. At any rate, the secretaries certainly did so, each changing things according to his own sense of what was required.

In the Department of the Interior, on the other hand, a change of approach in one program (the handling of Indian problems) did not interrupt the continuous existence of the main responsible agency— the old Office of Indian Affairs, which is a clear antecedent of today's Bureau of Indian Affairs. It did, however, bring down the Board of Indian Commissioners, set up in 1869 to distribute money to keep peace among the tribes. The board's mission was out of keeping with the more positive philosophy then taking hold, and the agency was terminated in 1933 in anticipation of a major overhaul of policy toward Indians the following year.

The end of the Diplomatic Bureau, the Consular Bureau, and the Director of the Consular Service in the State Department came from similar, but not identical, sources. There was widespread dissatisfaction with departmental performance during and after World War I. Highly politicized, inadequately financed, afflicted by incquities of salary and position, lacking presidential support, and surrounded by newly established rivals encroaching on its functions, the department was ripe for change. Wilson's secretary of state from 1915 to 1920, Robert Lansing, urged reorganization as he left office. Secretary Charles Evans Hughes cooperated with Congressman John J. Rogers in charting legislation. The measure became law in 1924, at which point the unified Foreign Service, operating on a merit system, replaced the venerable bureaus that had previously performed foreign relations services. New times, heavier workloads, and the need for greater competence took their toll through a process transcending party and personality.

Incapacity to meet new burdens also brought the end of two units in the Department of the Interior during the massive preparations for World War II. One was the Returns Office, a body created during the Civil War to promote honest contracting in the War, Navy, and Interior Departments by serving as a depository for their contracts. This quiet, routine operation was an anachronism in the milieu of total war. New agencies employing modern procedures were set up, and in 1941 a statute terminated it. In the same year, the War Minerals Relief Commission, established in 1919 to adjust the claims of firms that lost money producing or trying to produce certain minerals needed by the government during World War I, was abolished; presumably, if any claims were still pending, they would be handled by machinery adopted for similar purposes during the new conflict. The older organizations were simply overwhelmed.

Still another common cause of organizational death is the fusion of agencies separately established to perform specialized tasks that once were—or once seemed—unrelated but that turned out to impinge on one another, either because they expanded or because the unperceived linkages forced themselves on the consciousness of everyone involved. Take, for example, the Bureau of Lighthouses (begun in 1789), the Steamboat Inspection Service (1838), and the Bureau of Navigation (1884), all in the Department of Commerce at the time of their death. Each was set up to meet a particular need— warning ships of navigational hazards, increasing passenger and cargo safety, registering and licensing and regulating the merchant marine and merchant seamen. But they soon began to affect each other's work, and also the work of the Customs Bureau and the rapidly growing Coast Guard. In 1932 the Bureau of Navigation and Steamboat Inspection (later, Marine Inspection and Navigation) brought two of them together. In 1939 the Lighthouse Service disappeared into units of the Coast Guard operating the other navigational aids and services. And in 1942 the Bureau of Marine Inspection and Navigation was dismantled, its duties taken over by the Bureau of Customs and the Coast Guard, which by now were better equipped to perform them. The once discrete elements "grew together," and only the more vigorous ones retained their organizational identities.

Similarly, three organizations established as consequences of World War I were assimilated into larger entities engaged in almost identical operations. The War Transaction (or War Frauds) Section of the Department of Justice was set up after the war to prosecute people who had defrauded the government on war contracts. It was a program that could have been handled by other components of the department, and in 1926 the Claims Division took over its work. But its separate existence, even for a time, was a way of giving special emphasis to one type of offense, and it was allowed to lapse when the urgency passed. The Bureau of Industrial Housing, which became the U.S. Housing Corporation, was established in 1918 to liquidate housing run by the government in World War I. Eventually, it went to the Public Building Administration and then to the Federal Home Loan Bank Administration; in 1952 it was terminated by the secretary of the Home Loan Bank Board. Its unique functions had become nothing more than a small subdivision of much larger housing programs that eventually developed elsewhere in the governmental apparatus. So, too, ended the Fixed Nitrogen Research Laboratory, which got its chief impetus from military need for nitrates for munitions; it appeared first as a unit of the War Department in 1919. But the agricultural uses of nitrates for fertilizer were even greater in peacetime, so it was transferred to the Bureau of Soils, where its organizational identity disappeared when its War Department funds ran out. It was swallowed up by the larger research activities of which it was obviously a natural part.

In much the same way, the Supervising Architect of the Treasury Department was absorbed into the Public Buildings Branch of the department's Procurement Division, then into the Public Buildings Administration of the Federal Works Agency, and finally into the Public Buildings Service of the General Services Administration, where it gradually lost its distinctive organizational identity in a Division of Design and Construction. Also in the Treasury, the Division of Printing and Stationery was assimilated by the more general Division of Supply.

In the case of the Miscellaneous Division of the Department of the Interior, the transition was the other way; instead of vanishing into broader, more general agencies, its collection of disparate activities was slowly taken over by functionally specific units in the increasingly elaborate administrative services complex of the department. In 1950, forty-two years after its initial appearance, the last trace of it vanished. The Bureau of Foreign and Domestic Commerce, long a major component of the Commerce Department, also disappeared through the parceling out of its functions to other organizations, but in this instance the recipients included its own former constituents. Whereas the Miscellaneous Division was partitioned by external units, the bureau was assimilated in part by its own internal organs. There is doubtless an interesting story in this event, but the details are not recorded in the accessible public documents.

All the deaths taken together indicate that six of the seven anticipated hazards to organizational survival inventoried in chapter 1 do indeed prove fatal. Not all of them play a part in every fatality, of course; one or two suffice in most cases. Among the twenty-seven deaths, however, each of the hazards was a significant contributory factor in at least one case.

The one expected hazard that does not seem to have played a major role in any death is the alleged rigidity of statutes, which presumably would have impeded agency adjustments as conditions changed. I remarked earlier that this rigidity could cut either way, protecting agencies from casual elimination by actions less cumbersome than legislation or reducing their life expectancy by diminishing their adaptive capabilities. It has been shown that statutes do not contribute much to survival; now it appears they do not redound to the demise of agencies, either. If statutory origin were an obstacle to adaptation, deaths among statutory agencies would be proportionally higher than deaths among agencies set up by administrative action. But they were proportionally lower, constituting, as shown in table 4, only 56 percent of the deaths although statutory agencies made up 66 percent of the 1923 population. Obviously, statutory origin does not necessarily prevent government organizations from keeping up with the times. When organizations die, the explanation must lie elsewhere.

The major causes of death, in short, are competition, changes in leadership and policy, obsolescence resulting from routinization and adherence to past methods, and completion of mission. The increasing reorganizational powers of executive officers are also important; while, to an ever larger extent, they give rise to new agencies, they also facilitate the termination of existing ones. Only five of the twenty-seven deaths were accomplished by legislation. The others went by departmental action (eighteen), executive order (three), or reorganization plan (one). The forces sustaining the expiring agencies were not much in evidence; if Congress, allies, and clienteles took part in the final dramas, they did not leave a conspicuous record. The sources of agency autonomy did not shield these organizations from lethal factors.

Whether the age of an organization bears on its chances for survival is an open question. Comparing the ages in 1923 of the twenty-seven organizations that were to die in the next fifty years either with the age distribution of the entire 1923 population or with the age distribution of the organizations destined to survive yields proportions in each age class, despite some deviations, that are not markedly dissimilar (table 1, figure 3). The age of those that died ranged from 4 to 150 years, with cases pretty well scattered all along the ages between, at least to 109 years. Organizational death seemed to claim victims in all age categories without systematic discrimination.

There was, however, a faint tendency for the oldest organizations to fare better than their juniors, particularly the youngest (table 1). For example, 93 percent (14 out of 15) of the organizations one hundred years old or older in 1923 were still in existence in 1973; only 84 percent (134 out of 160) of the organizations under one hundred made the grade. Organizations under ten years old in 1923 were 20 percent of the total 1923 population, yet they made up nearly 30

FIGURE 3. *Age Distribution at Time of Death of Organizations
That Died between 1923 and 1973*

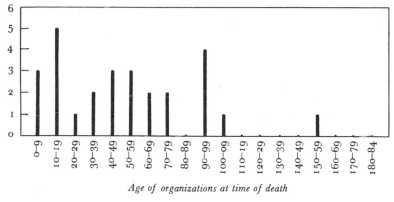

Number of organizations in each age group

Age of organizations at time of death

Source: Table 1.

percent of the group that died. The median age in 1923 of the 148 organizations that survived to 1973 was twenty-seven years, while the median age of those fated to die was just twenty-two years. Of the group that died, only 2 (less than 8 percent) were over a hundred at the time of their death, but 8 (30 percent) were under twenty. In 1923 organizations a century old or older were less than 9 percent of the sample; in 1973 they were more than 13 percent of a much larger sample.

Yet after all this, the really important question remains unanswered; though the data suggest reasons for the demise of the organizations that died, they do not tell us why these twenty-seven, rather than twenty-seven others with similar characteristics, succumbed. Were these twenty-seven subject to greater competition than the survivors? Were they afflicted by more extreme changes of leadership and policy? Were they victims of a deadlier obsolescence? Were they more rigid? Nothing indicates sharp distinctions between them and their more fortunate brethren, but the kind of detailed information about each unit is simply not at hand to confirm this impression. If, however, organizations resembling the fatalities survived while the hapless ones were going under, some factor not immediately discernible, or sheer chance, may be the reason.

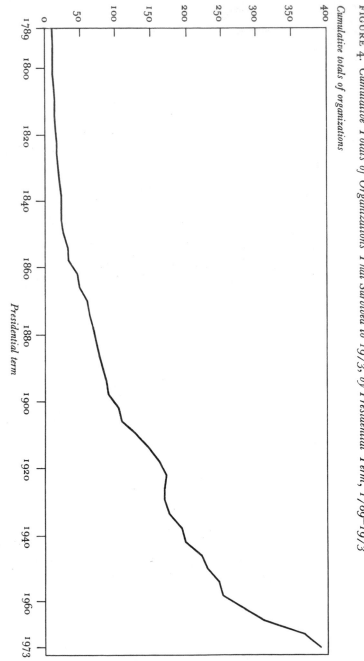

FIGURE 4. *Cumulative Totals of Organizations That Survived to 1973, by Presidential Term, 1789–1973*

Cumulative totals of organizations

Presidential term

Source: Table 6.

For example, the personal idiosyncrasies of leaders may be largely responsible. An executive disposed to take upon himself as many decisions as possible may kill off units. Another with a low tolerance for disorder and complexity will merge units merely to simplify organization charts. This is an intrinsically unpredictable variable on which the existence of agencies may depend. Perhaps one day such elements can be dealt with systematically. At present, all one can say is that they appear to occur randomly and make the probability of government units' dying exceedingly difficult to predict.

WHEN THE ORGANIZATIONS ALIVE IN 1973 ARE ARRANGED ACCORDING TO DATE OF BIRTH AND THE CUMULATIVE NUMBERS ALIVE IN EACH PRESIDENTIAL TERM ARE PLOTTED, THE CURVE PRODUCED ASSUMES AN EXPONENTIAL FORM (figure 4).

This finding is not a statement about population growth in the ordinary sense because it accumulates only organizations now alive according to their dates of creation; ordinarily, population figures for preceding periods include all units that were alive in each period even if they subsequently disappeared. It is therefore easy to misinterpret the finding, and it must be used with care, for it is really a still picture despite its time dimension.

Nevertheless, it is instructive. If trends exhibited from 1923 to 1973 were to continue, a series of subsequent still pictures of this kind would show still steeper slopes and higher totals than the 1973 picture, to the point where the vertical dimension of the graph would soon be much greater than the horizontal. Such a tendency bears some challenging implications for policymakers and managers of governmental machinery.

THE FINDINGS INTERPRETED

What do these findings tell us about the question of organizational immortality, to which this study is addressed? What do the data mean? Which of the two contradictory hypotheses about agency longevity is falsified? What are the implications for public administration and for policy formation?

ORGANIZATIONAL TURNOVER

Those who hold that government organizations enjoy great security and long life will discover in these findings ample support for their position. The impressive ability of agencies to stay alive once they have been launched is not mere conjecture.

What is more, it should be remembered that the functions performed by the agencies were even more enduring than the organizations themselves. In most of the twenty-seven deaths, the activities were not terminated; they were reassigned or taken up by other units, for the most part. The Board of Indian Commissioners and the Department of Agriculture's short-lived experiments with the directors of regulatory work and of scientific work may be classed as exceptions. And the post–World War I cleanup work of the War Frauds Section in the Department of Justice and the War Minerals Relief Commission of Interior was eventually declared finished. But as a general rule, once a service or program gets started, it seems to continue thereafter, just as conventional wisdom holds. Why this happens is no mystery; services and programs are instituted because they fill a need not otherwise met, whereupon people begin to count on them and to plan in the light of them. Terminating them would therefore cause hardship and even suffering, the effects of which radiate outward through the society. Added to the factors favoring continuation described in the first chapter, these social costs tip the balance against termination. Government officers dare not ignore them the way private interests can. Governmental activities therefore tend to go on indefinitely.

64

The persistence of functions and the indisputable hardiness of government organizations, however, should not be permitted to obscure the fact that agencies can and do die. Despite my determination to strain if necessary to find direct lineal descendants of the group in the 1923 sample, the number that petered out, though small, was not trivial. And if someday more frequent readings on the organizational population of the government are taken, there is reason to believe the death rate will turn out to be even higher. Even if it does not, however, and the prospects for survival remain as favorable as they now seem, an element of uncertainty about the future too large to ignore must be acknowledged.

The death of government organizations is important even though their functions are assumed by other units and continue after the organizations themselves disappear. After all, the same is true of private organizations; in the past, for example, many automobile manufacturers went out of business or sold out to other firms, but the production of cars did not stop. The characteristics of the industry and of its products, however, were surely shaped by these events, and the effects probably rippled through the whole transportation business and the society at large. The same is true in government. If, for example, consumer-oriented agencies die off and their functions are picked up by producer-oriented agencies, or if ecology-conscious agencies disappear while ecology-indifferent agencies in the same field flourish, the impact on public policy and on all the interests affected by public policy will not be negligible. And if organizations in the Executive Office of the President take over duties previously performed by departmental units, the shift in the center of gravity and power will hardly be inconsequential. Obviously, therefore, the appearance and dissolution of organizations in the public sector cannot be dismissed casually as of no importance—any more than they can in the private sector—just because functions outlive some of the agencies to which they were once entrusted.

Furthermore, quite apart from the immediate, practical consequences of organizational death, it has intriguing theoretical implications. A process of selective survival may be at work, in which case an evolutionary mechanism may be shaping the structure of the executive branch. The data here are not adequate to establish or disprove this possibility or to disclose how the selective principle, if there is one, works. But the fact that an endless turnover of organizations takes place, even at a modest rate, provokes speculation of a theoretical kind whose interest is only enhanced by the persistence of activities regardless of organizational death.

ORGANIZATIONAL BIRTH

Compared to the mysteries of organizational turnover, organizational birth is an open book. Agencies come into existence in response to demands for service from politically mobilized segments of society, both inside and outside the government. In many cases the services are assigned to new agencies rather than to old agencies in related fields, for the reasons described in the first chapter—distrust of the existing bodies and a strategy of assuring emphasis on a program by making it the exclusive concern of a separate body head the list. To these may be attributed the profuse growth in the number of federal agencies over the decades studied.

The tendency of births to come in clusters rather than in a steady stream is a bit harder to explain. Since differences in the personal attributes of various presidents play a large part, it is probably no accident that the periods of exceptional creativity more or less coincide with the tenure of presidents who showed vigor and imagination in other respects as well. Such presidents evidently seize upon needs and demands to fashion new programs and administrative bodies.

But the data indicate that the terms of some presidents *not* ordinarily noted for their inventiveness or aggressiveness were also periods of sharp increases in numbers of organizations—for example, the Taylor-Fillmore, Pierce, Grant, and Benjamin Harrison administrations, not to mention the Harding-Coolidge and first Eisenhower terms. This suggests that factors other than the personal qualities and political outlook of the chief executive, such as swings in economic conditions, aggravation of international tension, or achievement of international accord, spawn new agencies.[1] Even without such changes, the tide of creativity set in motion by a vigorous president apparently carries over into his successor's first term although his

1. In this connection, see the evidence that "the major stimulus to agency creation is a sudden shift in social, economic or technological change," in Carl Grafton, "The Creation of Federal Agencies," *Administration and Society*, vol. 7 (November 1975), pp. 328–65.

successor may be otherwise inactive. These inferences are consistent with the data.

Immersion in the data, however, suggests another factor that cannot be deduced from the numbers. It is a kind of "spontaneous creation" of new units—spontaneous in the sense that it is governed by the internal dynamics of organizational life rather than by calculations and overall plan. The incessant, uncontrived division and subdivision of work gives many units their start.

To be specific, individuals in any organization gravitate toward particular sectors of activity unobtrusively and perhaps unconsciously. By virtue of this specialization, they become more adept at these tasks than their fellows are. Gradually, they come to know the regulations, the essential contacts, the admissible shortcuts, the files, and the pitfalls of the areas they work in. Problems are routed to them. Their advice is sought. They become acknowledged, indispensable resources. Eventually, it is regarded as unseemly that such prized personnel should spend their valuable time on routine chores, so they are given (or use their bargaining power to insist upon) assistance, freeing them for greater participation in high level planning and deciding. As a matter of convenience, what has thus become a group is identified in organization charts, procedural manuals, and telephone directories. The leader, by reason of seniority as well as achievement, is granted appropriate title, rank, salary, and status. Thus a new organizational unit has emerged. Within it, in turn, the process continues, branches and sections forming slowly and pushing the original leadership post to still higher levels. From the bottom, then, as well as from the top, organizational growth in administrative structures goes on little by little.

If this is true, the process will take place willy-nilly. It is invariably impelled by increasing workloads. Population growth alone would produce some additional workload, so that pressure is always exerted. But such things as technological advances and economic growth add to the pressure; they engender specialization and the establishment of separate units of specialists. Observers are prone to attribute these tendencies to the empire-building proclivities of bureaucrats, and there is little doubt that bureaucrats at all levels love to carve out their own secure little niches. At bottom, though, there seems to be a "built-in" thrust that encourages and assists the ever finer division of labor in organizations. Out of that come more organizations, products of a series of developments so small they are hardly noticed individually as they occur. Collectively, if this hypothesis is valid, these insignificant changes could transform administrative structures without anyone ever having made a single, major, deliberate decision to alter them. Much of the growth observed in this study seems to have occurred this way. It may have been hastened or slowed by a favorable or hostile presidential administration or perhaps by other chance factors, which accounts for the spurts and clusters. The driving force, however, is inherent and unremitting.

ORGANIZATIONAL DEATH

Organizational deaths are harder to explain. Although it is easy enough to offer plausible after-the-fact reasons for each of the 27 fatalities in the sample of 421, the differences between this batch of 27 and other organizations that survived cannot be detected by the limited means available for this study.

Nevertheless, some aspects of the data invite speculation. If the weak advantage of the oldest organizations over others in resisting death is not just an artifact of method or a peculiarity of the sample examined, can it be explained? One hypothesis, consistent with common impressions, is that although organizations become more rigid as they grow older their environment in the administrative system is so stable as to sustain fixed patterns while destroying more flexible, experimental organizations. That is, doing essentially what was always done—not rocking the boat or making waves—could have survival value in this setting, so older, more inflexible organizations would fare very well.

On the other hand, it is by no means self-evident that the federal administrative system *is* as unchanging as this hypothesis requires. The list of hazards to agency survival suggests the opposite, and the rapid rise in the number of new organizations in the sample, whatever its origin, surely constitutes a set of environmental changes of no small magnitude. If all organizations, as is generally believed, become less flexible as they age, older ones ought to experience a higher death rate than young ones in such a setting. The fact that they do not—that they do a little better, if anything—casts doubt on the allegation of inevitable sclerosis. Organizational old age does not seem invariably to bring on greater rigidity.

Rather, age may affect different organizations in different ways. Suppose some organizations are in the classical mold and stiffen as they grow older; in a dynamic environment, they would die off as their capacity to adapt declined (which, if each stiffens at its own pace, would account for the occurrence of deaths in all age classes). Suppose also that some are rigid from the moment of establishment; they would not last long (which may be why there is a relatively high death rate among younger organizations). And suppose finally that some are flexible from the start or grow flexible over the years; they would survive for a long time in a continuously changing setting. The system would "select out" all but the most flexible, and old age would indicate great adaptability, not great rigidity.

All these hypotheses about organizations and their environment fit together because each focuses on a part of the organizational world. As a general rule, the constantly changing environment may screen out all but the most flexible organizations. At the same time, a few rigid ones may fall into stable environmental "niches," where they could endure for long periods despite their limitations. As a result, the oldest group would comprise both very flexible and very rigid organizations (though the former would predominate because unchanging niches are rare in dynamic systems). From time to time, a shift impinging on a niche or an accumulation of rigid tendencies would cause the death of an organization even in the oldest group; no organization would be immune. On balance, then, the prospects for those that are fortunate enough to persist for long periods would be bright, unlike the prospects for old organisms.[3] And all the data would be accounted for.

2. Herbert Kaufman, "The Natural History of Human Organizations," *Administration and Society*, vol. 8 (August 1975), pp. 131–49.

3. Anthony Downs concluded this must be the case in *Inside Bureaucracy* (Little, Brown, 1967): "The older a bureau is, the less likely it is to die" (p. 20). Samuel P. Huntington advanced the same conclusion in *Political Order in Changing Societies* (Yale University Press, 1968): "The older an organization is, the more likely it is to continue to exist through any specified future time period" (p. 13). See also Herbert Kaufman, *The Limits of Organizational Change* (University of Alabama Press, 1971), pp. 99–100. All of these assertions are reasoned inferences; they are not based on any adduced empirical evidence.

In this connection, it may be worth noting that no cabinet-level department has ever gone out of existence. The War and Navy Departments were demoted to subcabinet status when the Department of Defense was created, and the Post Office Department was made an independent agency instead of an executive department, but they certainly retained their organizational identities despite these changes. It is therefore possible that more ferment and turnover occur at lower levels than at higher ones. It is even possible that the turnover at any level is proportional to its distance from the top. (The parallel to the root system of a tree suggests itself, but such metaphors must be viewed skeptically.) The most obvious explanations for the differences are that administrators are able to make changes more readily than Congress and that lower levels can act more readily than high ones because the impact of their actions is so localized. But this line of speculation goes far beyond what the data warrant.

Whichever, if any, of the foregoing hypotheses turns out to be accurate, one thing is not in much doubt: public officers of the future will have to deal with larger numbers of organizations than do their counterparts today, and many of these abundant organizations— probably an increasing proportion of the total—will be extremely long-lived.

CAN THE NUMBER OF AGENCIES BE CONTROLLED?

Explosive growth in the number of units in the public administrative system and intensification of the attendant problems, described at the beginning of this book, are evidently approaching rapidly—if in fact they have not already arrived. For example, suppose the number of units in a sample comparable to this one in 2023 bears the same ratio to the 1973 population that the 1973 population bears to the 1923 group. The 2023 organizational sample would then consist of 887 units, including 333 survivors from 1973 and 554 created in the five decades following.

That is an extreme assumption. For such an expansion to come about, the rate as well as the absolute number of births would have to go up dramatically—from fewer than 5 a year in 1924–73 to more than 11 a year in 1974–2023, not even counting those that appear and then disappear between readings. Growth of this kind is far from inconceivable, to be sure; in the 1874–1923 period the comparable annual rate was only 2.3 units a year, and since it doubled in the next half-century, there is no a priori reason that it could not double again. Still, it is a radical expectation.

But the figures are striking even if much more conservative assumptions are made. Suppose in the departments studied the number of organizations created in the course of the next fifty years and surviving to the end of the period should attain a rate only 50 percent higher than in the previous fifty years, or 7.4 a year. By 2023 that would have added 370 to the population, which, combined with the anticipated 333 carry-overs from 1973, would produce a total of 703 units in the group comparable to the one covered in this study.

Indeed, if you project continued growth at the *same* rate that applied in the half-century ending in 1973—a very cautious estimate— the total number of organizations in the group would be 579— 333 long-lived carryovers, 246 new ones.

Alarming as these figures are to some students of administration, there are others who question whether the numbers need really worry us at all. They believe the concern about them is based on false premises.

For one thing, the perceived trends may not continue. Straight-line extrapolations into the future are always risky, especially when, as in this case, they rest on relatively few observations. Moreover, all sorts of self-limiting factors may come into play and check past tendencies.

For another thing, even if past trends do continue, the capacity to deal with them may increase commensurately. Maybe new managerial methods will be conceived, new analytic techniques devised, new technology invented, or new structures assembled to keep pace with the presumed stresses besetting the system. Or maybe people in such a trying environment would behave differently from people today and the troubles anticipated by applying today's standards to tomorrow's world will never materialize.

Furthermore, an untidy aggregation of organizations in government may be no cause for uneasiness. Attempting to cram the complexity and diversity of political institutions into a preconceived and rather arbitrary pattern of symmetry and simplicity and neatness, it could be argued, would do more violence to the system and generate more disorder than allowing it to establish its own untidy format. Perhaps it will evolve into a special kind of marketplace, with its own equilibria, or eventually reach a ceiling, as most growing populations do. For managerial purposes, the notion that governments are structurally identical to organisms may be misleading.

These are powerful arguments. When the pains and consequences of an expected illness are exaggerated, drastic preventives and remedies more injurious than the ailment itself may be taken. Still, it can do no harm to *think* about what might be done if it should become plain that the ailment is serious. The reasons recounted earlier for suspecting this might be the case cannot be dismissed out of hand. Rejecting Cassandra need not mean embracing Pangloss or Pollyanna. It is therefore appropriate to ask: if we wanted to hold down the organizational population in government, what could we do?

Fundamentally, there are only two levers to control the size and average age of any population: births and deaths. Were it within one person's power to adjust these rates at will, that person could set the levers to achieve whatever effect he or she wanted. More births than deaths would increase size; more deaths than births would reduce it. A balance of high birth and death rates would produce a stable, young population; one of low rates would yield a stable, older population. Variations in the sizes of the excesses, the blends of the rates, and the timing of equilibria could generate whatever state of affairs the manipulator wanted. All that with just two levers.

Birth control. Limiting the birth rate of public agencies is not a mere figure of speech in the public arena; several states have actually adopted provisions to their constitutions setting upper bounds on the number of departments that may be established in their respective governments.[4] To say the principal purpose of these provisions is to

4. The New York State constitution names nineteen departments and forbids the legislature to create new ones (though it may *reduce* the number). Other states specify the maximum number of departments but do not name them. One names some departments and authorizes not more than five additional ones. Nebraska sets up four by constitutional provision and requires a two-thirds vote of the entire membership of the legislature to create more. See Legislative Drafting Research Fund of Columbia University, *Index Digest of State Constitutions*, 2d ed. (Oceana, 1959), pp. 471–73; Council of State Governments, *The Book of the States* (Lexington, Ky.: biennial), sec. 4, p. 1.

restrict the number of government organizations would be an exaggeration; in most cases, the object is to hold down each governor's span of control, and the creation of bureaus lodged within the permitted departments has not been banned—nor has it been retarded. Nevertheless, this reaction to the continuous expansion of the number of organizational units in the states is a straw in the wind, and could conceivably lead to attempts to set limits *within* departments as well as upon departments as a strategy of desperation by opponents of governmental growth. Critics from all bands of the political spectrum, for different reasons but with equal fervor, denounce bureaucracy. Someday this could result in an extension of the policy of agency birth control.

Increasing the death rate of federal organizations. As for the second lever, three ways of elevating the organizational death rate have from time to time been advanced.

The oldest and most familiar formula is the proposal to transfer the functions of federal agencies to private organizations or to state and local governments.[5] Traditionally, this has been a politically conservative position, formulated and defended by people who distrust and oppose governmental activity on ideological grounds. Its basic premise, however, has been endorsed by many who regard themselves as liberals and who do not share this aversion to governmental expansion; revenue sharing has been justified by some of its most ardent sponsors as a method of transferring fiscal resources to the government levels at which they can be most effectively employed.[6] If the federal government were to heed these recommendations religiously, one result would certainly be the demise of many federal administrative organizations (though new organizations would probably spring up outside the federal administrative structure to receive the transferred responsibilities).

The second prescription for raising the death rate of federal organizations is to limit the period during which statutes (and other in-

---

5. Peter Drucker, *The Age of Discontinuity* (Harper and Row, 1968), pp. 234–42, on "reprivatization"; Gordon Tullock, *The Politics of Bureaucracy* (Public Affairs Press, 1965), pp. 221–24.

6. Walter W. Heller and Joseph A. Pechman, *Questions and Answers in Revenue Sharing* (Brookings Institution, 1967), p. 12.

struments of creation) setting up agencies remain valid.[7] At present, most enabling laws are of indefinite duration, remaining effective until they are repealed. Some commentators believe this practice provides sanctuaries where units that have lost their effectiveness and their raison d'être are permitted to continue. If every unit were compelled periodically to undergo the same review and self-justification it was subjected to originally, presumably some would survive by upgrading themselves, but many would be unable to vindicate themselves and would be allowed to expire. In this fashion, the administrative system would be pruned.

The third suggested way of elevating the death rate of organizations is to intensify competition by simulating the marketplace, thereby harshening the governmental environment and building up

7. Theodore J. Lowi, *The End of Liberalism* (Norton, 1969), pp. 309–10, calls for a "limit of from five to ten years on the life of every organic act" creating an agency. Justice William O. Douglas, *Go East, Young Man* (Random House, 1974), p. 294, declares, "The great creative work of a federal agency must be done in the first decade of its existence if it is to be done at all. After that, it is likely to become a prisoner of bureaucracy and of the inertia demanded by the Establishment of any respected agency. This is why I told FDR over and over again that every agency he created should be abolished in ten years. And since he might not be around to dissolve it, he should insert in the basic charter of the agency a provision for its termination." The *Washington Post* of November 23, 1975, agreed editorially: "Virtually all units of government, no matter how noble their purposes or how vigorous their first few years may be, grow stale and soft eventually. Congress now tends to fight this bureaucratic aging process by heckling agencies, poking at them, issuing more directives and demanding more reports— while voting them more money to pay for more personnel and more activity. But such unsystematic oversight is likely to produce more paperwork than progress. It makes more sense to write expiration dates into the laws, thus forcing administrators to justify their work—and legislators to rethink their purposes—in an orderly way every few years."

These proposals are not empty rhetoric. On November 6, 1975, Representative Max Baucus succeeded in attaching to a bill setting up a consumer protection agency (H.R. 7575, 94 Cong. 1 sess., subsequently vetoed successfully by President Ford) an amendment providing for the expiration of the agency after seven years unless specific action to continue it were taken by the President and Congress. Moreover, Representative Abner Mikva, on December 18, 1975, introduced for himself and two dozen colleagues the "Regulatory Agency Self-Destruct Act" (H.R. 11278, 94 Cong. 1 sess.) applying similar provisions to nine other agencies as well.

"natural" forces that weed out the less hardy units.[8] Although every federal organization already faces competition, often from several sources, the market-simulation technique would give the *consumers* of public services free choice among agencies rendering essentially identical services, much the way consumers can choose among essentially similar automobile manufacturers; at present, competition in the administrative system does not take this form. Were such a plan adopted, it would probably raise the level of organizational mortality substantially.

Improbability of success. For good or ill, the prospects for adopting these methods of limiting the number of organizations do not seem bright. And the likelihood that all of them would work as expected if they were adopted seems doubtful.

As regards "birth control," everybody will approve blocking the appearance of organizations advocated by others but will oppose impediments to the ones they themselves want. In such a situation, logrolling is the highly predictable outcome. People will bargain and will therefore not press objections to proposals advanced by others if the others will return the favor. Political participants at all levels, including bureaucracies, will also actively support programs and agencies in which they have little interest to secure backing for the ones they are keenly concerned about. Logrolling added to the other factors engendering the birth of new organizations in the federal system would produce a formidable combination of forces. The result would surely be the perforation of any ceiling on agency numbers if one should ever be imposed.

Nor do I see much promise in measures to raise the organizational death rate. Shifting functions from federal agencies to other institutions, public or private, may lead temporarily to the dissolution of some units. However, as inconsistencies of policy and practice among the separate and scattered substitutes emerged, as states and localities experienced the traumata of augmented burdens on already strained fiscal resources, as groups whose constitutional rights had been infringed sought redress in a more responsive arena, and as local political and economic interests demonstrated they are not free of many

8. For example, see Anthony Downs, "Competition and Community Schools," in Henry M. Levin, ed., *Community Control of Schools* (Brookings Institution, 1970), pp. 219–49.

of the ills of federal administration and are subject to deficiencies of their own as well, demands for renewed federal surveillance and control and even for direct federal administration would multiply. New units would be set up to respond to the clamor. Whatever organizational terminations were induced by transferring functions would thus be offset by the births it engendered. The character of the organizational population would change in some ways (not necessarily for the better), but after a short while, the net mortality rate and the number of units in the system would not.

They would not be reduced by imposing time limits on agency-enabling legislation, either. Such time limits may have other effects, but controlling organizational population would not be one of them because the costs of the practice would be intolerable. Imagine the paralysis, the sense of suspended animation, that would overtake agencies, their clients, and their beneficiaries as expiration dates approached. Think of trying to do business and plan for the future under such conditions. Visualize the dilatory tactics of interests that, having lost an immediate battle over federal intervention, strove to delay implementation until the automatic reopening of the struggle rolled around. And finally, consider the crush and confusion in legislatures as they tried in each session both to dispose of current business and to renegotiate the accumulating body of prior settlements. Time limits would soon be abandoned or ignored. Organizations would be routinely and uncritically renewed. Things would soon revert to their present state.

Simulating the marketplace in the public administrative arena would probably enjoy no greater success. After all, the public turned from the economic market to the government for certain services and protection because the market failed to provide these benefits at an acceptable price when they were wanted.[9] To turn government into the mechanism already judged inadequate (instead of preserving an alternative to that mechanism) is a prescription that would not sit well with many people. The production of public goods often suffers if reliance is placed on individual instead of collective action.[10] No one would deny that there are costs and inefficiencies associated with

9. Wallace S. Sayre and Herbert Kaufman, *Governing New York City* (Norton, 1965), pp. 59–62.

10. Mancur Olson, Jr., *The Logic of Collective Action* (Harvard University Press, 1965), pp. 165–67.

government operations, but there are also costs in letting the market-place try to respond to people's needs and wishes. The growth of government is strong evidence of the willingness of most people in the country to bear the costs of government as well as of the marketplace. These values may change, but there is no reason to anticipate a dramatic reversal in the years immediately ahead.

It appears to me, then, that neither lowering the birth rate nor raising the death rate of federal administrative organizations is likely to succeed as a strategy for controlling the organizational population. Whatever lies ahead, the only course open seems to go on as before. If the optimists are right, the future will be no worse than the present. If the pessimists are right, all we can do is brace ourselves for what is to come.

HOW LITTLE IS KNOWN

To have to close with such an inconclusive assessment of the future and such a dearth of policy proposals is disappointing. But there is some value in these defects because they highlight how little is known in the area studied. One of the purposes of publishing this study is to call attention to this gap. Despite the limitations of time and re-sources that confined the inquiry to very narrow grounds and to vague conclusions, the effort will be vindicated if it provokes other students of administration and of organization theory to venture deeper into this uncharted area.[11]

In particular, more studies of the deaths of organizations are needed. Most of the literature on organizations is derived from the experience of successful cases. This preoccupation is natural when one is searching for paths to success, which is what most management

11. As these words were written, a list of births and deaths of federal organiza-tions from 1960 to 1973 was being assembled by the Congressional Research Service; Sharon S. Gressler and James McGrath, "Federal Agencies, Commis-sions, Bureaus and Departments Created or Terminated between 1960 and 1973 on a Year by Year Basis" (Washington, 1974; processed). The criteria for inclu-sion on that list and for determining organizational death were not the same as those adopted for this study; nevertheless, the data point toward the same im-pressive powers of organizational endurance noted in this inquiry. Like this inquiry, however, the list is only a first, small, uncertain step that raises more questions than it answers. The journey has barely begun.

literature is concerned with; what better route to this end than to examine and emulate winners? But one must understand sickness and death to understand health; pathology contains many of the clues to normality. Information about failure is wanting in the study of public administration.

Also required is much more information about the aggregation of organizations encompassed in the federal administrative structure than it was possible to assemble and analyze in this study. More readings, coverage of agencies excluded for reasons of convenience and economy, and more complete and reliable historical data are needed—in short, a much more complete and dependable record.

Gathering such information is not a simple matter. It is laborious, costly, and time-consuming. It will take a long while to put together enough data for reliable analysis. The payoffs are uncertain.

In the circumstances, it is hardly worthwhile to try to reconstruct the past—at this stage, anyway. It would be much easier to begin with the present and carry the record-keeping forward from this point on. The current organization of the executive branch can be captured in a brief, intensive effort; thereafter, updating it would be a routine and relatively modest operation. The data would accumulate almost automatically.

Although years would elapse before enough data piled up to yield fresh theoretical insight into the dynamics of the organizational population, the data being accumulated might serve as useful management tools long before that. It would be possible to array the administrative structure of the executive branch, or of any parts of it, in computer printouts on a moment's notice. Managers could even experiment with various kinds of reorganization and trace out some of the consequences on computers before putting new arrangements into effect. By adding some details about personnel and program, the production of the *Government Manual* could be partly, if not wholly, automated. Introducing time series on budgets, staffing, payrolls, and workloads would facilitate comparative administrative analysis. Eventually, the history of individual units could be summoned up in short order.

Perhaps these side benefits would be enough to offset the costs of data collection. In the end, however, the justification for such an enterprise resides in its contribution to organization theory. Nobody can guarantee the outcome. All we have is reason to hope that deeper understanding of the behavior of organizational populations will enable us to do more than merely cope with the problems population growth promises to present; the new understanding may empower us to surmount those problems, make them routine, and lift our capacity to master the administrative challenges and opportunities now bearing down upon us.